THE CHARACTER OF
THE FIVE-FOLD
MINISTRY

Through the Lens of LOVE

LEON D. NELSON JR.

Printed in the United States of America

First Printing, June 2020

ISBN Print
ISBN: 978-1-7338770-3-9

EMBASSY MINISTRIES INTERNATIONAL INCORPORATED

THE CHARACTER OF
THE FIVE-FOLD MINISTRY

Through the Lens of LOVE

Hello My Fellow Yokemen

The Word is SELAH! Pause and think about it.

Let me tell you about the Golden Bridge on the cover.

The Golden Bridge is the connection between your gift and your character. Let's look at the Word to meditate on first before you begin this adventure with the teacher, the coach, the mediator, The Holy Spirit.

Romans 11:29. 29For God's gift and His call are irrevocable. [He never withdraws them when once they are given, and He does not change His mind about those to whom He gives His grace or to whom He sends His call.]

Proverb 18:16. 16A man's gift makes room for him and brings him before great men.

Ephesians 4:11-13. 11And His gifts were [varied; He Himself appointed and gave men to us] some to be apostles, (special messengers), some prophets (inspired preachers and expounders), some evangelists (preachers of the Gospel, traveling missionaries), some pastor (shepherds of His flock) and teachers. 12His intention was the perfecting and the full equipping of the saints (His consecrated people), that they should do] the work of ministering toward building up Christ's body (the church), 13[That it might develop] until we all attain oneness in the faith and in the comprehension of the [full and accurate] knowledge of t he Son of God, that [we might arrive] at really mature manhood (the completeness of personality which is nothing less than the standard height of Christ's own perfection), the measure of the stature of the fullness of the Christ and the completeness found in Him.

I Peter 4:10-11. ¹⁰As each of you has received a gift (a particular spiritual talent, a gracious divine endowment), employ it for one another as [befits] good trustees of God's many-sided grace [faithful stewards of the extremely diverse powers and gifts granted to Christians by unmerited favor]. ¹¹Whoever speaks, [let him do it as one who utters] oracles of God; whoever renders service, [let him do it] as with the strength which God furnishes abundantly, so that in all things God may be glorified through Jesus Christ (the Messiah). To Him be the glory and dominion forever and ever (through endless ages). Amen (so be it).

As you take time with the Holy Spirit, He will begin to develop the character of Christ Jesus that will sustain the gift. As you allow the Holy Spirit to grow you up in His gracious anointing, His character will protect the grace, and you will never compromise your position. Your time with the Holy Spirit will be your key your continuous progress in skillful, Godly wisdom and revelation of who you are in Christ and your assignment.

So let's agree. Say this out loud with me:

Heavenly Father, thank You for Jesus; Lord Jesus thank You for Your willingness to call me to represent You in Your office. I yield to the Holy Spirit to teach, and lead, and guide me to have the character to compliment Your gift that You have given me. I am ready to hear clearly and to respond correctly like never before. AMEN.

Now Let's Get Started!

CONTENTS

FOREWORD

I AM DELIGHTED TO WRITE this Foreword because Apostle Leon Nelson has been My Spiritual Father and Co-Laborer in Christ for more than twenty years. He has made a tremendous impact on my life as a man of God, a loving husband, a caring father and a compassionate Pastor. I often say I would not be where I am today if it had not been for the GOD VOICE in him for me. I love you so much Dad! Always continue to teach and train the disciples that God sends you to be led by your voice here on the earth.

In my 27 years of ministry I have never heard such revelation of the Five-Fold Ministry offices. I believe deeply in the content in this book, especially in the character of each fivefold office. My Dad, Apostle Nelson, makes the teaching of the fivefold offices crystal clear; he explains in detail through the Word of God how the fivefold should operate.

The simplicity of the teaching in this book is amazing, especially the emphasis on the character of the office, not just from the perspective of the gifts of the office. He brings home the benefits of the fivefold to the body of Christ and provides wisdom and insight for the body of believers in order to strive for maturity and growth into the fullness of Christ.

Apostle Leon Nelson describes the office of the Teacher as the "cream of the crop" and recounts from two unique perceptions why the Teacher is given this honor. The first is the exclusive role of the Holy Spirit in training the Teacher to raise disciples that will make a difference in our modern world, distinguishing themselves by living the kingdom lifestyle.

He then calls attention to the respect accorded the Teacher by society and the community in raising men, who can be used by God for the edifying of the saints.

My Dad then teaches about the office of the Pastor next to the Teacher. He identifies the Pastor as the one who nourishes the flock, grooming them for Jesus Christ. And, one notable calling in the primary responsibilities of the Pastor is intercession.

The office of the Evangelist follows in chapter three. Apostle Nelson describes the Evangelist as the "Father's Dinner Bell of Love," seeking and ushering into the kingdom the new beginnings. Hence, the Evangelist mirrors the love of Christ and demonstrates the heart of God's longing for souls.

His exposition gives clarity to the full understanding of all five offices, and inspires the seamless flow of creativity in grasping the concept.

Apostle Gregory McCurry
New Beginning Ministries
New Beginning Fellowship International

THE FIVE-FOLD MINISTRY IN YOUR PALM

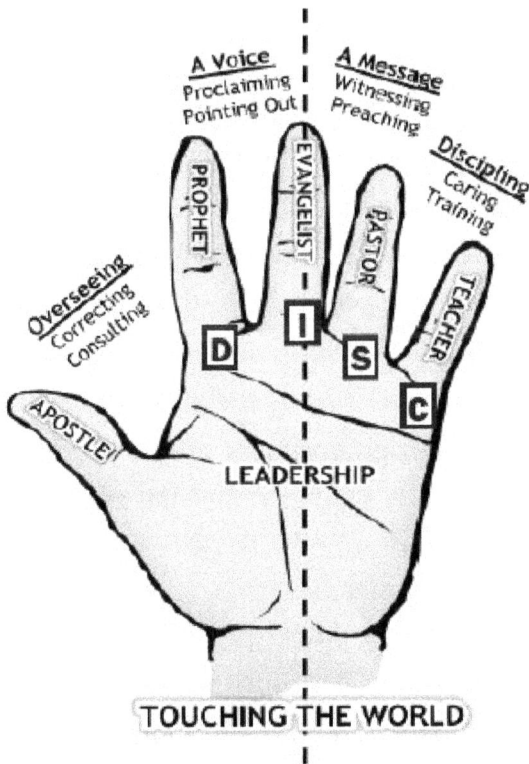

A Voice
Proclaiming
Pointing Out

A Message
Witnessing
Preaching

Discipling
Caring
Training

PROPHET

EVANGELIST

PASTOR

TEACHER

Overseeing
Correcting
Consulting

APOSTLE

D

I

S

C

LEADERSHIP

TOUCHING THE WORLD

I T WAS A PLEASURE gathering my thoughts together on this topic for this new and exciting book that speaks on the Five-Fold ministry – the character of Christ and the gifts that touch the world. I believe that we are working from the Father's mandate which He gave to us through the Lord Jesus Christ – that we should teach the ministry gifts, emphasizing the character of the office that goes with the gift.

> **Mark 16:15 AMPC**
> *And He said to them, Go into all the world and preach and publish openly the good news (the Gospel) to every creature [of the whole human race].*

We receive our mandate from the Word of God, and the same Word also empowers us.

In this book, our focus is on the character of the Five-Fold ministry officers within God's perfect plan to divide the work in His House into five distinct branches. We are thus gifted and should work hand-in-hand with these ministries for the equipping of the saints and the empowering of the Kingdom of God on earth.

Indeed, God planned to see the offices operating out of godly character – the righteousness of Christ, revealed in the Gospel by which God is seen as both Just, and the Justifier of the one that believes in Jesus.

> **Psalm 119:7 AMPC**
> *I will praise and give thanks to You with uprightness of heart when I learn [by sanctified experiences] Your righteous judgments [Your decisions against and punishments for particular lines of thought and conduct].*

Now the precepts of the one and the doctrines of the other are to be learned and developed for each office, as the Father teaches in His word and by His Spirit. The practice and experience of them then become part of the individual's personality.

The goal of the development of character of the Five-Fold Ministry is to have the mind of Christ. For every facet of the five-fold office expresses the character of Christ, which is the fruit of the Spirit:

Galatians 5:22-23 AMPC

But the fruit of the [Holy] Spirit [the work which His presence within accomplishes] is love, joy (gladness), peace, patience (an even temper, forbearance), kindness, goodness (benevolence), faithfulness, Gentleness (meekness, humility), self-control (self-restraint, continence). Against such things there is no law [that can bring a charge].

The fruit is seen as we grow in each office and put on the armor of God as instructed in Ephesians 4:11; 6:11-17. The gifts of the Spirit will also flow as we spend time renewing our mind

Philippians 2:5 AMPC

Let this same attitude and purpose and [humble] mind be in you which was in Christ Jesus: [Let Him be your example in humility].

We need to adopt the mind of Christ in all offices, and all office holders must display the character of Christ

Romans 12:1-2 AMPC

I appeal to you therefore, brethren, and beg of you in view of [all] the mercies of God, to make a decisive dedication of your bodies [presenting all your members and faculties] as a living sacrifice, holy (devoted, consecrated) and well pleasing to God, which is your reasonable (rational, intelligent) service and spiritual worship. Do not be conformed to this world (this age), [fashioned after and adapted to its external, superficial customs], but be transformed (changed) by the [entire] renewal of your mind [by its new ideals and its new attitude], so that you may prove [for yourselves] what is the good and acceptable and perfect will of God, even the thing which is good and acceptable and perfect [in His sight for you].

As Five-Fold ministry officers, it is we who will set the tone that will enable the whole world to be saved and live in unity. This can only be done through the character of Christ that we display, and the acts of love we demonstrate through Jesus Christ, our Lord.

We ought to understand as well that Jesus Christ Himself had a plan to make this work seamless, ensuring a steady progression, from the time we are saved to the time we are ready for ministry. This is where the Five-Fold Ministry comes into operation, where men and women of God are positioned to hold different offices (of leadership) in the house of God, so that successive generations of believers can recognize the vision and the character of the Father in the leaders as they grow in the House of God.

Let me give you a portion of the scripture that introduces the subject of this book more comprehensively.

Ephesians 4:7-16 AMPC

Yet grace (God's unmerited favor) was given to each of us individually [not indiscriminately, but in different ways] in proportion to the measure of Christ's [rich and bounteous] gift. Therefore it is said, When He ascended on high, He led captivity captive [He led a train of vanquished foes] and He bestowed gifts on men.

[But He ascended?] Now what can this, He ascended, mean but that He had previously descended from [the heights of] heaven into [the depths], the lower parts of the earth? He Who descended is the [very] same as He Who also has ascended high above all the heavens, that He [His presence] might fill all things (the whole universe, from the lowest to the highest). And His gifts were [varied; He Himself appointed and gave men to us] some to be apostles (special messengers), some prophets (inspired preachers and expounders), some evangelists (preachers of the gospel, traveling missionaries), some pastors (shepherds of his flock) and teachers. His intention was the perfecting and the full equipping of the saints (His consecrated people), [that they should do] the work of ministering toward building up Christ's body (the church),

[That it might develop] until we all attain oneness in the faith and in the comprehension of the [full and accurate] knowledge of the Son of God, that [we might arrive] at really mature manhood (the completeness of personality which is nothing less than the standard height of Christ's own perfection), the measure of the stature of the fullness of the Christ and the completeness found in Him.

So then, we may no longer be children, tossed [like ships] to and fro between chance gusts of teaching and wavering with every changing wind of doctrine, [the prey of] the cunning and cleverness of unscrupulous men, [gamblers engaged] in every shifting form of trickery in inventing errors to mislead. Rather, let our lives lovingly express truth [in all things, speaking truly, dealing truly, living truly]. Enfolded in love, let us grow up in every way and in all things into Him Who is the Head, [even] Christ (the Messiah, the Anointed One). For because of Him the whole body (the church, in all its various parts), closely joined and firmly knit together by the joints and ligaments with which it is supplied, when each part [with power adapted to its need] is working properly [in all its functions], grows to full maturity, building itself up in love.

Verse 11 of the above scriptures reveals five distinct ministries in: The Apostle, The Prophet, The Evangelist, The Pastor, and The Teacher. All these work in concert in the same body of believers, providing leadership in different spheres for the perfecting of the character of the gifts.

All ministries originate from Jesus Christ. In his letter to the Ephesians, the Apostle Paul introduced us to the Five-Fold ministry, also known as "The Ascension Gift Ministries" because we received them when Christ ascended into heaven [verse 8]. I like the timing of this gift – *as soon as* Christ ascended into heaven. The reason behind this was the fact that Christ, in His mission, designated humankind as the ones who would carry on His work after He left the earth.

However, this could only be achieved after He had lived for some time among the disciples, teaching them as many things about the Kingdom as were possible at that time. And, after seeing Him demonstrate His mission right before their eyes, they were ready when the time was ripe to handle the different ministries.

When reading the gospel of John, we see that Jesus Christ took time out to go and pray alone. In most of those prayers, He always talked about how He wanted the Holy Spirit to be with the people He was going to leave behind. He wanted them to carry on with the work that He had started, therefore revealing that it was always His plan to leave His people working as different ministers in the House of God.

The appointment of these various ministries is also what we have inherited up to this day. We have inherited the same ministries from the ones that walked with Christ and had continued with the work of the ministry when He had ascended to heaven. It follows that every person in the Body of Christ has received grace to carry out some aspect of the Five-Fold Ministry offices. In whatever we do, whatever we touch and produce, please understand the Holy Spirit is fine-tuning your character the office. The office is perfect but your character has to be molded for your maturity through the process of discipleship.

It is He that we should acknowledge at all times. These are just some of the things to remember because many times we see people straying away from the purposes of God. They develop pride, behaving as if they are succeeding because of their own brilliance; yet it is God who gifts people in their callings.

Zechariah 4:6-7 AMPC

Then he said to me, This [addition of the bowl to the candlestick, causing it to yield a ceaseless supply of oil from the olive trees] is the word of the Lord to Zerubbabel, saying, Not by might, nor by power, but by My Spirit [of Whom the oil is a symbol], says the Lord of hosts. For who are you, O great mountain [of human obstacles]? Before Zerubbabel [who with Joshua had led the return of the exiles from Babylon and was undertaking the rebuilding of the temple, before him] you shall become a plain [a

*mere molehill]! And he shall bring forth the finishing gable
stone [of the new temple] with loud shoutings of the people,
crying, Grace, grace to it!*

God spoke through the Prophet Zechariah to Zerubbabel, letting
him know that it was not by his power that the mountain before
him should become a plain. This could only happen by the Spirit
of God and by His grace. The same power is with us to this day –
God enables ministers among us to minister mightily. Thus His
Spirit and grace should be acknowledged as the chief drivers of
the work of the ministry, not the people who are doing it for God.

We indeed appreciate the Grace of God when we look at
all dimensions of the Five-Fold Ministry. We see this in the gift of
prophecy and the Prophet. It also applies to the apostolic
anointing and the Apostle, the pastoral anointing and the Pastor,
and others alike. Grace reigns supreme, and this should never
escape our minds – that all we do has been made possible by the
grace of God and not our human wisdom.

The key to understanding the Five-Fold Ministry is in the
words "FUNCTION" and "PURPOSE," not the title in itself. The
title is there to describe the FUNCTION and thus should not be
made the sole focus, especially for the ones who hold the title. The
title holders should make it a point to write in their hearts that
the functions that come with the title are their sole focus. More
so, it is not only the title holders who need help with refocusing
their attention on the office and the ministry to the congregation,
but all of us. That is all a part of our character development. We
should see nobody but Jesus ... All too often we have problems
when we shift our focus to the title bearer and lose our focus on

the Father who is the Great Gifter behind everyone's fruitfulness in ministry.

For the sake of a better understanding of the functions of each office in the five-fold ministry, I have researched these definitions:

The **Apostle** Governs: He is like the Heart revealing compassion and the strategy for advancing the Kingdom.

The **Prophet** Guides: He is like The Mouth, communicating guidance. He takes his words from God and reveals them to the congregation.

The **Teacher** Grounds: He has the Mind of Christ to bring wisdom and understanding to the people; and he does so patiently to help everyone understand the purpose of the message.

The **Evangelist** Gathers: These are the Hands that are always reaching out to souls for their salvation. Once they bring souls in, they are delivered to the Pastors and Teachers for further guarding and grounding in the Word of God.

The **Pastor** Guards: These are the Feet leading the sheep to pasture and the paths of righteousness. Their work is continuous, and thus Pastors are forever present in the lives of believers, providing guidance every step of the way.

Our hand (as in the image on the first page) serves as an interesting example of the Five-Fold Ministry, too:

The **Thumb** represents the Apostle: this finger is the only one that touches all the others and is the one that enables us to have a grip on something.

The **Forefinger** represents the Prophet: its purpose is to point towards a certain direction. The function of pointing is not just about pointing, but the pointing is done so that it can be followed by an action. This action is the one that takes believers in the same direction in which the "finger" is pointing.

The **Middle finger** represents the Evangelist: it has the furthest reach – "go out into all the world."

The **Ring finger** represents the Pastor: he is married to the sheep, always with them.

The **Pinky** represents the Teacher: this finger is the one that gives balance and stability to the hand.

The 5 Gs of Ministry

The Apostles and Prophets lay the foundation of the House. The Teacher builds on that foundation with the stones that the Evangelist gathers, and then the Pastor cares for the House. The "House," of course, means the people of God.

The Apostle "Governs" or oversees the House, bringing vision, order, and government. They develop leaders and raise "sons in the Gospel."

The Prophet "Guides" and administrates in the House. They declare and confirm the vision for the House and operations. They also bring direction and counsel.

The Teacher "Grounds" and equips the saints through their gifted teaching of the word. They bring balance to the vision of the House.

The Evangelist "Gathers" by training workers/witnesses to reach out to the community.

The Pastor "Guards" the House, caring for the people, overseeing visitations, organizing prayer and intercession, and many others. They are concerned with the everyday aspects of the community of faith.

As such, the 5 Ascension Gift Ministries function together as a Team so that all the ministry functions can be channeled to the betterment of the House of God, with believers complementing one another's efforts.

We can also go further into the functions of each Ministry because the work is extremely vast as part of an organized Kingdom. Here are some other services of each Ministry:

The Apostle is to look "Godward" and minister to Him. As they do, they receive the vision, and then they go and plow the ground for the "harvest."

The Prophet has, what we would call, a "watchman on the wall" or "crow's nest" ministry.

The Teacher grounds as they reemphasize the vision of the House and consolidate it in the Word. They break up the fallow ground.

The Evangelist gathers the people and also sows seeds.

The Pastor guards by example, leading the prayer and care ministries and harvesting the crop.

Are all Ministries Equal?

Although each Ascension Gift Ministry is vital to the Church, it is essential to realize there is a "governmental" aspect to Ministry. We see this in one of Paul's letters where he speaks about the Five-Fold Ministry:

1 Corinthians 12:28 AMPC

So God has appointed some in the church [for His own use]: first apostles (special messengers); second prophets (inspired preachers and expounders); third teachers; then wonder-workers; then those with ability to heal the sick; helpers; administrators; [speakers in] different (unknown) tongues.

The Apostle is primary, the Prophet secondary and the Teacher is third. All are equal in the fact that each one is a member of the Body of Christ. But there is "order" and "government" in the ministries, too. The Apostle is guarded by the other four because his anointing is the "primary" anointing.

***

When speaking of the five offices that Jesus Christ gifted us with, we ought to emphasize the importance of unity as a binding force. This ensures a smooth flow of tasks that believers are engaged in, from the work of the Evangelist to that of the Teacher, and so forth.

We now turn to Ephesians 4:7-16 that introduces the Five-Fold Ministry and, naturally, I would like to explain a few words that are in these same scriptures. A portion of verse 7 speaks of the grace that has been given to all of us, individually: "***But unto every one of us is given grace according to the measure of the gift of Christ***" (KJV). When I see the word "grace," I am always brought to think of how much every one of us was saved from our past sins. As a result, I have a simple definition from the Lord about grace: "Grace is the ability of the Holy Spirit given to us to do His will."

Romans 3:23-24 AMPC

Since all have sinned and are falling short of the honor and glory which God bestows and receives.

[All] are justified and made upright and in right standing with God, freely and gratuitously by His grace (His unmerited favor and mercy), through the redemption which is [provided] in Christ Jesus ...

The grace of God was availed to us to redeem us from the death that awaited us. In that grace, there was the process of attaining and upholding the same grace for the rest of your life. That process would involve several people that God would send into your life as different ministers. This is the reason why, when the Five-Fold ministry is being introduced, we see the word "grace" mentioned and said to have been given to every "one of us" as individuals. This emphasizes the plan of God, that in everything that He does for you and me, the idea is always to save us from eternal destruction and defeat through His abundant grace.

When we understand the difference between law and grace, we will recognize that the purpose of the five-fold ministry is to retrain all disciples to learn how to depend on the Holy Spirit for the strength to enjoy the new creation's kingdom lifestyle.

Moving on to the other verses in Ephesians Chapter 4, we see that in verse 12, it is God's intention to perfect and fully equip the saints for the journey ahead. This equipping of the saints is to give us the enabling to do the work of the ministry towards building up the body of Christ.

Therefore, when you get saved, you will ultimately take up some work in the ministry. However, this has to follow specific processes in which ministers who are set apart by God take you through the different phases of your Christian journey.

When these different ministers take you through these processes, they will be fulfilling their callings according to how they are gifted within the realm of the five-fold ministry.

Moving ahead, verse 13 reveals to us the ultimate aim of the different ministries that are placed among us to help us grow the body of Christ into one. Growth to that extent considers several factors such as spiritual growth that nurtures a high level of tolerance. This is absolutely necessary since working in the Kingdom of God involves many people who come from different backgrounds and with different attitudes.

The more we understand the function of the five-fold, the more we will see how the Holy Spirit is key to growth in the disciple-building process.

Above all, the five-fold ministry represents leadership. Leadership started from Old Testament times when God placed Adam and Eve in the Garden of Eden and gave the man a dominant role.

When you look into it, you will observe at least five leadership roles God assigned to His people in the Old Testament:

1. Covenant bearers – Abraham, Isaac, Jacob
2. Divinely appointed trail blazers – Moses, Joshua
3. Priests – Aaron, Levites
4. Judges – Deborah, Gideon, Samson
5. Kings – Saul, David
6. Prophets – Isaiah, Jeremiah, Ezekiel

The above-listed leadership roles were dispensed across the Old Testament right from the start, with the Covenant Bearers in the Book of Genesis to the Prophets, who made up the last portion of the Old Testament. Soon after the Prophets, we see the emergence of John the Baptist, who came more in the role of a Prophet preparing the way for the soon-coming Messiah (Isaiah 40:3-5; Malachi 3:1; Matthew 3:3; Mark 1:3; Luke 3:4-6).

These scriptures reveal the importance of this prophetic office in the five-fold even as the gospel confirmed the coming of Jesus Christ as heralded by John the Baptist. Of all the leadership eras I highlighted coming from the Old Testament, there is so much to learn. All these leaders were part of some extraordinary events characterized by God's direct communication with His people.

Communication is always at the heart of our relationship with God, and this is how we keep in touch with the heavens all the time. In the past, there were Prophets, and Abraham had several encounters with God, such that God called him His friend. Communication with the Holy Spirit is our key to having continuous growth. And in this, we enjoy greater blessing than anyone in the Old Testament because of the precious Holy Spirit dwelling in us.

2 Chronicles 20:7 AMPC

Did not You, O our God, drive out the inhabitants of this land before Your people Israel and give it forever to the descendants of Abraham Your friend?

My desire is to impress on those in the five-fold ministry that the unity of the faith comes because Jesus Christ has already forged that in the Spirit on behalf of the Body of Christ. We now have the Holy Spirit to ensure that the will of the Father will be continuously carried out through the body in which successive generations of disciples are being loved and taught. We must not discount the work of the Holy Spirit in the perfecting of the saints or, to be more accurate, the disciples.

> **Psalm 133:1-3 AMPC**
> *Behold, how good and how pleasant it is for brethren to dwell together in unity!*
>
> *It is like the precious ointment poured on the head, that ran down on the beard, even the beard of Aaron [the first high priest], that came down upon the collar and skirts of his garments [consecrating the whole body].*
>
> *It is like the dew of [lofty] Mount Hermon and the dew that comes on the hills of Zion; for there the Lord has commanded the blessing, even life forevermore [upon the high and the lowly].*

Unity of purpose in the body or house makes everything else flow, and this is the desire of any church leadership. We can see from Psalm 133 how unity is compared to the oil flowing down the body of Aaron, from his head down to the hem of his garment. The flow of oil is a good analogy as, by just observation, you discover quite a few interesting things. Notice how the oil particles roll over each other to create that smooth flow. In other words, brethren in the church do well when they depend on each other for movement. Once there is a lack of the unity of purpose, the flow stops. This is the stage that the five-fold ministry fails to deliver on its mandate, resulting in a church of spiritual dwarfs.

In our new relationship with the Holy Spirit, everything in ministry can be made even smoother because the leading of the Holy Spirit is the key to the success of the growth of the disciples.

The second observation is how slow the flow of oil is. It is quite different from water. Why is a slow flow good? Well, I understand how people are not happy when things seem to get stuck and slow-paced. However, when speaking of growth in Christ to the point where a person is ready to lead in the House of God, it takes a lot of effort. This involves learning many lessons from several ministers God has chosen and anointed for us in the order of the five-fold.

To understand unity, you must know that the Holy Spirit is the oil. And the person of the Holy Spirit knows exactly how to move with the five-fold like He did with Jesus. We must not forget the role of the Holy Spirit in the growth of the disciples.

Now that we understand what the Five-Fold Ministry offices are, and that they work well when believers are living together in harmony, we can go ahead and examine each of the Ministries in a deeper way. Remember that God has blessed us with these ministries so that they may help in the building up of the Body of Christ.

This leaves you with something to think about. Whether you are a church member, a minister or you are aspiring to be involved in the five-old ministry, I would like you to ask yourself if what you are doing daily is helping the body of Christ to grow.

THE CHARACTER OF THE
FIVE-FOLD MINISTRY

L♥VE

Through the Lens of

CHAPTER ONE

THE TEACHER - THE CREAM OF THE CROP

I HAVE ALWAYS HAD A particular interest in the Teacher. The Teacher is the person who explains things, and trust me, this is not an easy thing to do. However, God always enables the ones that He anoints such that they will not find it difficult to impart knowledge to His people whenever they set themselves to do it.

I call the Teacher the "Cream of the Crop" because of the nature of the Holy Spirit in him. It is He who has been training the Teacher to teach the disciple to live the kingdom lifestyle in the world, and to be the light and salt.

I also call the Teacher the Cream of the Crop because even society out there knows that the title comes with much respect. I am speaking not only in terms of what happens in church, but also about what happens in our communities where children, and even adults, spend considerable portions of their days in a class, with a teacher speaking to them about different life subjects and imparting the spirit of excellence.

The Vision and the Teacher

The vision of the office must tie into the vision of the house, and we must look at Character, not personality. Character is the place of submission to be used by the Holy Spirit. When I speak of vision I am talking about Redemptive revelation.

> **Proverbs 29:18 AMPC**
> *Where there is no vision [no redemptive revelation of God],*
> *the people perish; but he who keeps the law [of God, which*
> *includes that of man]—blessed (happy, fortunate, and*
> *enviable) is he.*

Most disciples have a God-given dream that must be connected to a God-given vision. When the disciple is taught to put the Father's vision first, then their personal dream will become their personal testimony, which will always manifest. And their testimony will be an evangelistic tool to win the world one person at a time.

Most people have a dream that is personal to the individual ... for that dream to come to pass, it must be connected to a vision for the house.

Teachers represent an investment in knowledge, and the world knows well that the attainment of knowledge equals the realization of power. When believers are knowledgeable about the Father's purpose, including all His love, then the Ministry grows strong every day, and this indeed pleases God. As the Teacher is led by the Holy Spirit, the disciple will begin to develop a kingdom mindset, which is totally different from that of the world. The new mindset will develop the mind of Christ that is vital to living the kingdom lifestyle. In the world the Teacher has the anointing to do that with the help of the Holy Spirit.

Now, going back to the House of God, in as much as we are taught to treat everyone as equals, it is imperative to understand that in a church, we are not equal. We are different in terms of what we can give, and how fast we respond to the messages being preached every week in church. Some of us are seasoned – strong in the word, and others are babes in Christ – just learning the word. Yet we all desire to be more like Christ through working with the Teacher of the word of God.

1 Thessalonians 5:14 AMPC
And we earnestly beseech you, brethren, admonish (warn and seriously advise) those who are out of line [the loafers, the disorderly, and the unruly]; encourage the timid and fainthearted, help and give your support to the weak souls, [and] be very patient with everybody [always keeping your temper].

Therefore, since some of us come short in many areas, Teachers of the Word of God are there to close this gap by helping the weak to soar and reach new heights like everyone else.

We have in place the office of Teacher to allow the Holy Spirit to teach through them to us so as to bring the disciple to the place of growth, Remember, the Teacher has that combination of love and patience to help the disciple to grow like never before.

In imparting knowledge, the Teacher employs certain listening strategies that resonate well with disciples who are still lacking in confidence in what they are capable of doing. When someone pays attention to your talk, even if it sounds shallow, you grow in confidence and would want to share more about your experiences. It is quite the opposite when you try to say something in front of an unruly audience and all they do is respond with laughter, mocking whatever you are trying to put across.

It is a different story with Teachers. They pay attention to everything you have to say showing empathy and understanding from where you are coming. They use this knowledge to elicit the help of the Holy Spirit to select just the right knowledge to the disciples, and when He does, growth will be guaranteed. Again, this indeed pleases the Father.

Teachers also help us understand things that appear complex on the surface. They are there to help unlock specific hidden meanings that do not make sense when we try to look at them at the first go. More so, Teachers help us unlock the potential that is in us because they invest a lot of time in making sure that we understand ourselves better; your character determines why you do what you do and act the way you act. The disciple learns by revelation given by the Teacher that causes it to become real to them. Therefore, because of the Teachers in the House of the Lord, many ministers who are gifted in other areas of the five-fold ministry are identified, encouraged and groomed towards taking up their positions – as called by God.

Overall, Teachers are very dedicated ministers. Even in the Body of Christ, they invest much time in preparing their lessons, sometimes weeks. They buy many teaching aids with their own money and all this they do with their disciples in mind. They take time to learn how their disciples absorb information and go ahead and buy the items that they think can accelerate this. This shows us that Teachers think about their disciples even when in their homes – something that is amazing and shows such great passion.

Again, just like the Pastor, a Teacher has an important place in the maturing of the saints. The Teacher is that part of Jesus that makes sure that the disciples will grow up into the burden-removing, yoke-destroying lifestyle of the Kingdom Citizen (Ephesians 4:11-13; James 3:1-2).

The Teacher has that final grace upon them to allow the much-needed patience to have its perfect work through them for the benefit of the manifestation of the mature saint, who will live the Kingdom Lifestyle in their world.

The anointing of love and patience is the grace on the Teacher that will cause the disciple to walk into their FULL SONSHIP – Maturity. Why the anointing of love on the Teacher? This takes us back to what we have just mentioned in the previous paragraphs: that the Teacher dedicates most of their time and some personal resources to help the disciple, even in their absence. This is the manifestation of the gift of love for others.

The Teacher makes the truth and knowledge about God accessible to all. But it is quite imperative to know that it also takes all five-fold ministry offices to perfect the Church of God.

> **Ephesians 4:11-13 AMPC**
> *And His gifts were [varied; He Himself appointed and gave men to us] some to be apostles (special messengers), some prophets (inspired preachers and expounders), some evangelists (preachers of the gospel, traveling missionaries), some pastors (shepherds of His flock) and teachers.*
>
> *His intention was the perfecting and the full equipping of the saints (His consecrated people), [that they should do] the work of ministering toward building up Christ's body (the church),*
>
> *[That it might develop] until we all attain oneness in the faith and in the comprehension of the [[a]full and accurate] knowledge of the Son of God, that [we might arrive] at*

really mature manhood (the completeness of personality which is nothing less than the standard height of Christ's own perfection), the measure of the stature of the fullness of the Christ and the completeness found in Him.

By its very nature, the Ministry Office of the Teacher is primarily to the already saved. However, anointed instruction in the Scriptures can also have a powerful evangelistic effect.

Psalm 51:13 KJV
Then will I teach transgressors thy ways; and sinners shall be converted unto thee.

Like the other four ministry offices, the Teacher helps believers come to *"the unity of the faith – [to] the knowledge of the Son of God - unto a perfect man"* of Ephesians 4:13, to a Christian maturity, pursuing the perfect example of Jesus Christ. Keywords in this are the "unity" of faith and "helping" believers come to God. Teachers help, and they do so passionately, making them an essential addition to the Body of Christ.

The Teacher Will Be Judged More Strictly

Now, this sounds rather severe, but even so, it is understandable in the Kingdom of God. I say this because God, in the Old Testament, was strict with His people and the commands that He gave them. When He spoke, they had to obey or else some judgment was going to be laid on them.

However, when it comes to God judging the Teachers more strictly than the rest, it has something to do with them knowing the rules of God better than anyone else. For no one can teach what he does not understand, or is not thoroughly knowledgeable of. So, we are merely saying that becoming a Teacher of the word of God must be a ministry for the ones who are called to it, who will give it the respect it deserves.

James 3:1-2 AMPC

Not many [of you] should become teachers ([a]self-constituted censors and reprovers of others), my brethren, for you know that we [teachers] will be judged by a higher standard and with greater severity [than other people; thus we assume the greater accountability and the more condemnation].

For we all often stumble and fall and offend in many things. And if anyone does not offend in speech [never says the wrong things], he is a fully developed character and a perfect man, able to control his whole body and to curb his entire nature.

Again, I want to bring you back the point that brethren are supposed to dwell together in unity so that these five-fold ministers can produce the fruits they are called to do out of their work. When the children of God are not pulling in the same direction, the Spirit of God will not be among them for the simple reason that God will not be pleased. He does not dwell where there is strife. The Teacher has the anointing to eliminate the spirit of strife.

Psalm 133:1-3 AMPC

Behold, how good and how pleasant it is for brethren to dwell together in unity!

It is like the precious ointment poured on the head, that ran down on the beard, even the beard of Aaron [the first high priest], that came down upon the collar and skirts of his garments [consecrating the whole body].

It is like the dew of [lofty] Mount Hermon and the dew that comes on the hills of Zion; for there the Lord has commanded the blessing, even life forevermore [upon the high and the lowly].

The Character of the Teacher

Understanding the office of the Teacher helps believers understand who they are, and this reduces the likelihood of strife between them and other ministers and believers. Their nature comes from God.

Exodus 4:12 AMPC

Now therefore go, and I will be with your mouth and will teach you what you shall say.

Galatians 5:22-23 AMPC

But the fruit of the [Holy] Spirit [the work which His presence within accomplishes] is love, joy (gladness), peace, patience (an even temper, forbearance), kindness, goodness (benevolence), faithfulness, gentleness (meekness, humility), self-control (self-restraint, continence). Against such things there is no law [that can bring a charge].

The nature of the Teacher is such that they will act upon the words that are put by God in their mouths. They also will be living proof of the fruit of the Spirit as they will live with love, joy, peace, and happiness. They will face the class bearing these.

Jesus Christ Too Was a Teacher

At some point in scripture, Jesus was called "the Great Teacher" by people who knew about His work. He also spoke about the characteristics that determine the one that shall be called "great" in the Kingdom of God. Below are a few scriptures that speak of Jesus' role as a great Teacher of the Word of God.

Matthew 5:19-20 AMPC

Whoever then breaks or does away with or relaxes one of the least [important] of these commandments and teaches men so shall be called least [important] in the kingdom of heaven, but he who practices them and teaches others to do so shall be called great in the kingdom of heaven.

For I tell you, unless your righteousness (your uprightness and your right standing with God) is more than that of the scribes and Pharisees, you will never enter the kingdom of heaven.

Matthew 11:1-2 AMPC

When Jesus had finished His charge to His twelve disciples, He left there to teach and to preach in their [Galilean] cities.

Now when John in prison heard about the activities of Christ, he sent a message by his disciples.

Matthew 8:19 AMPC

And a scribe came up and said to Him, Master, I will accompany You wherever You go.

Mark 4:1 AMPC

Again Jesus began to teach beside the lake. And a very great crowd gathered about Him, so that He got into a ship in order to sit in it on the sea, and the whole crowd was at the lakeside on the shore.

The Holy Spirit Will Teach You

The lessons in the Bible are not always about helping believers go through their Christian journeys. They are also about teaching people how to deport themselves in specific life situations. In these situations we hear the Lord promising believers that the Holy Spirit (who by the way is the same as God the Father and the Son) will teach them what to say at a specific hour and a specific situation.

Luke 12:12 AMPC

For the Holy Spirit will teach you in that very hour and moment what [you] ought to say.

John 14:26-27 AMPC

But the Comforter (Counselor, Helper, Intercessor, Advocate, Strengthener, Standby), the Holy Spirit, Whom the Father will send in My name [in My place, to represent Me and act on My behalf], He will teach you all things. And He will cause you to recall (will remind you of, bring to your remembrance) everything I have told you.

Peace I leave with you; My [own] peace I now give and bequeath to you. Not as the world gives do I give to you. Do not let your hearts be troubled, neither let them be afraid. [Stop allowing yourselves to be agitated and disturbed; and do not permit yourselves to be fearful and intimidated and cowardly and unsettled.]

Below, are more Bible verses so that you can read and understand more on the subject of Jesus and the Holy Spirit being our Teachers, too. The Holy Spirit even helps in the appointment of ministers in church.

Acts 1:1 AMPC

In the former account [which I prepared], O Theophilus, I made [a continuous report] dealing with all the things which Jesus began to do and to teach

Acts 20:27-28 AMPC

For I never shrank or kept back or fell short from declaring to you the whole purpose and plan and counsel of God.

Take care and be on guard for yourselves and the whole flock over which the Holy Spirit has appointed you bishops and guardians, to shepherd (tend and feed and guide) the church of the Lord or of God which He obtained for Himself [buying it and saving it for Himself] with His own blood.

Acts 20:32 AMPC

And now [brethren], I commit you to God [I deposit you in His charge, entrusting you to His protection and care]. And I commend you to the Word of His grace [to the commands and counsels and promises of His unmerited favor]. It is able to build you up and to give you [your rightful] inheritance among all God's set-apart ones (those consecrated, purified, and transformed of soul).

Acts 20:35 AMPC

*In everything I have pointed out to you [by example] that,
by working diligently in this manner, we ought to assist the
weak, being mindful of the words of the Lord Jesus, how He
Himself said, it is more blessed (makes one happier and
more to be envied) to give than to receive.*

Jesus Christ Sat under Teachers, Too

As I mentioned before, Christianity is a journey that starts when
one is born again. From there, the believer goes through a process
that sees them coming under the counsel of different ministers
in church. This is how they grow because the ultimate aim is for
them to minister in their due season.

The purpose of learning under a Teacher is to grow. Even the
Lord Jesus learned under His elders when He was young. You
may raise questions on why He had to do this since He knew
everything about the Kingdom of His Father. But His mission on
Earth was to show us the way, which indeed included learning
under others and a teachable spirit. Thus, He spent time in the
temple when he was still young, learning from the books and
the elders.

He also learned to show obedience to His Father through
experiential learning and suffering, so that obedience might be
passed down to us, too. You will find the following scriptures very
instructional. They talk about obedience, humility, relationship
and submission to the will of the Father that laid the foundation
for His anointing and powerful intercession.

Hebrews 5:8-14 AMPC

Although He was a Son, He learned [active, special] obedience through what He suffered

And, [His completed experience] making Him perfectly [equipped], He became the Author and Source of eternal salvation to all those who give heed and obey Him,

Being designated and recognized and saluted by God as High Priest after the order (with the rank) of Melchizedek.

Concerning this we have much to say which is hard to explain, since you have become dull in your [spiritual] hearing and sluggish [even slothful in achieving spiritual insight].

For even though by this time you ought to be teaching others, you actually need someone to teach you over again the very first principles of God's Word. You have come to need milk, not solid food.

For everyone who continues to feed on milk is obviously inexperience and unskilled in the doctrine of righteousness (of conformity to the divine will in purpose, thought, and action), for he is a mere infant [not able to talk yet]!

But solid food is for full-grown men, for those whose sensed and mental faculties are trained by practice to discriminate and distinguish between what is evil and contrary either to divine or human law.

1 John 2:27 AMPC

But as for you, the anointing (the sacred appointment, the unction) which you received from Him abides [permanently] in you; [so] then you have no need that anyone should instruct you. But just as His anointing teaches you concerning everything and is true and is no falsehood, so you must abide in (live in, never depart from) Him [being rooted in Him, knit to Him], just as [His anointing] has taught you [to do].

Hebrews 7:25-26 AMPC

*Therefore He is able also to save to the uttermost (completely, perfectly, finally, and for all time and eternity) those who come to God through Him, since He is always living to make petition to God and intercede with Him and intervene for them. [Here is] the High Priest [perfectly adapted] to our needs, as was fitting—holy, blameless, unstained by sin, separated from sinners, and exalted higher than the **heavens**.*

We are Called to Become Fully Mature Christians

As we spoke about Teachers among Christians, we have also presented how much God wants us to grow in the Kingdom. No Christian will mature in isolation in the absence of the Teachers and other ministries that help pump in the life that Jesus expects from His followers. Therefore, until we mature in Him, the Teacher will be there to continue to encourage the disciple.

Colossians 1:27-28 AMPC

To whom God was pleased to make known how great for the Gentiles are the riches of the glory of this mystery, which is Christ within and among you, the Hope of [realizing the] glory. Him we preach and proclaim, warning and admonishing everyone and instructing everyone in all wisdom (comprehensive insight into the ways and purposes of God), that we may present every person mature (full-grown, fully initiated, complete, and perfect) in Christ (the Anointed One).

Beware of False Teachers! Don't Accept Just anyone who Comes Along with some Exciting or New Thing!

As we conclude this chapter, I realize how important it is to leave a word of wisdom for you. Here's a warning. Not everyone who comes to you in the name of Jesus is for Him. Neither is everyone who comes presenting something exciting while holding a Bible in their hands true, and coming in the name of the True God. There are false teachers out here, and you ought to stay vigilant so as not to be swayed.

2 Peter 2:1-3 AMPC

But also [in those days] there arose false Prophets among the people, just as there will be false teachers among yourselves, who will subtly and stealthily introduce heretical doctrines (destructive heresies), even denying and disowning the Master Who bought them, bringing upon themselves swift destruction. And many will follow their immoral ways and lascivious doings; because of them the true Way will be maligned and defamed. And in their covetousness (lust, greed) they will exploit you with false (cunning) arguments. From of old the sentence [of condemnation] for them has not been idle; their destruction (eternal misery) has not been asleep.

Teach with Integrity, Seriousness, and Soundness of Speech

Teaching the word of God is not something we can afford to take lightly. We are talking about life for all eternity and should thus give it the utmost respect. Therefore, when you are asked to teach, you ought to do so in all seriousness and integrity.

The Teacher who has been taught by the Holy Spirit will walk in the level of integrity that the Holy Spirit will develop because the Spirit of Christ Jesus lives in the Teacher.

> **Titus 2:7-8 AMPC**
>
> *And show your own self in all respects to be a pattern and a model of good deeds and works, teaching what is unadulterated, showing gravity [having the strictest regard for truth and purity of motive], with dignity and seriousness.*
>
> *And let your instruction be sound and fit and wise and wholesome, vigorous and irrefutable and above censure, so that the opponent may be put to shame, finding nothing discrediting or evil to say about us.*

A good Bible Teacher will impart the truth in such a way that his hearers will receive it as biblically sound teaching and will apply it to their lives without any hesitation.

> **2 Timothy 1:13 AMPC**
>
> *Hold fast and follow the pattern of wholesome and sound teaching which you have heard from me, in [all] the faith and love which are [for us] in Christ Jesus.*

2 Timothy 2:2 AMPC

And the [instructions] which you have heard from me along with many witnesses, transmit and entrust [as a deposit] to reliable and faithful men who will be competent and qualified to teach others also.

1 Corinthians 4:17-18 AMPC

For this very cause I sent to you Timothy, who is my beloved and trustworthy child in the Lord, who will recall to your minds my methods of proceeding and course of conduct and way of life in Christ, such as I teach everywhere in each of the churches. Some of you have become conceited and arrogant and pretentious, counting on my not coming to you.

2 Timothy 3:10 AMPC

Now you have closely observed and diligently followed my teaching, conduct, purpose in life, faith, patience, love, steadfastness,

The Teacher, too (and all Christians, for that matter) can be used to perform supernatural signs as Jesus was recognized to have done as a Teacher.

John 3:2 AMPC

Who came to Jesus at night and said to Him, Rabbi, we know and are certain that You have come from God [as] a teacher; for no one can do these signs (these wonderworks, these miracles—and produce the proofs) that You do unless God is with him.

Need to close with a strong word of exhortation.

THE CHARACTER OF THE FIVE-FOLD MINISTRY

Through the Lens of

L♥VE

CHAPTER TWO

THE PASTOR - YOUR NOURISHER

THE WORD "PASTOR" COMES from the same word in Latin which means "shepherd." The New Testament presents two offices that constitute church leadership: the elder, who is also known as the overseer and deacon. We will look at these two qualifications for elder/overseer later in the chapter. But first I feel compelled to share a deep revelation that the Lord gave me for the Pastor.

The Word of the Lord to the Pastor – to My Nourisher

"The time has come to display how tender and loving and kind I am; and that I have chosen and ordained and picked you out to move through you, like never before. It's My choice; it's My office and I have picked you out to represent Me. I will cause you to know Me by revelation now. I am about to show you who you are to Me, and as My nourisher.

"I will feed, guide and shield you and you will not lack My wisdom, My knowledge and My understanding as you are My light to My sheep. They are My sheep and I have called you to be like Me for them. I have given you My

voice, and they will follow My voice speaking through you. Your time with Me is crucial now. I know everything about My sheep, and I will trust you with them. Your time with Me will allow Me to give you all that you will ever need for My sheep as they receive all that they will desire to grow and grow and grow.

"Remember, I have already ordained you for My position with My sheep. I have given you My ability to be a Good Shepherd for Me. There will never be any lack in My ministry. I am your source of everything you will ever need or desire to make sure that My sheep are always taken care of. I trust you; that's why I picked you out and gave you all that you will ever want or desire to bring Me glory. I will bring to remembrance and supply you with everything you will need to bring My will to pass.

"Never forget, it's My will that I have called you to help Me fulfill. I am ready and I have molded you, so Come On and Go With Me!"

How the Father Sees the Pastor – You

The Father always looks to the end product and therefore sees you as His finished piece.

John 14:12-14 AMPC

I assure you, most solemnly I tell you, if anyone steadfastly believes in Me, he will himself be able to do the things that I do; and he will do even greater things than these, because I go to the Father. And I will do [I Myself will grant] whatever you ask in My Name [as presenting all

*that I Am], so that the Father may be glorified and extolled
in (through) the Son. [Yes] I will grant [I Myself will do for
you] whatever you shall ask in My Name [as presenting
all that I Am].*

I want you to see how God see you and how you really are. Perhaps
due to life's challenges, you can develop an erroneous perception
about yourself. Even though the Lord shows you who you are, it
doesn't change your opinion. But it is so crucial in the character
intended for you to understand how He sees you. If you allow
God to minister to you about your divine identity and how He
sees you to the point where you agree with Him, then the level
of confidence that you begin to have in who He says you are will
be simply amazing.

The Pastor and the Office

The office of the Pastor is so important that we are going to
examine the following two scriptures and more, as we go into
a deeper understanding of their significance, definition, and
functions.

I Timothy 3:1-7 AMPC
*The saying is true and irrefutable: If any man [eagerly] seeks
the office of bishop (superintendent, overseer), he desires
an excellent task (work). Now a bishop (superintendent,
overseer) must give no grounds for accusation but must
be above reproach, the husband of one wife, circumspect
and temperate and self-controlled; [he must be] sensible
and well behaved and dignified and lead an orderly
(disciplined) life; [he must be] hospitable [showing love*

for and being a friend to the believers, especially strangers or foreigners, and be] a capable and qualified teacher, not given to wine, not combative but gentle and considerate, not quarrelsome but forbearing and peaceable, and not a lover of money [insatiable for wealth and ready to obtain it by questionable means]. He must rule his own household well, keeping his children under control, with true dignity, commanding their respect in every way and keeping them respectful. For if a man does not know how to rule his own household, how is he to take care of the church of God? He must not be a new convert, or he may [develop a beclouded and stupid state of mind] as the result of pride [be blinded by conceit, and] fall into the condemnation that the devil [once] did. Furthermore, he must have a good reputation and be well thought of by those outside [the church], lest he become involved in slander and incur reproach and fall into the devil's trap.

Titus 1:5-9 AMPC

For this reason I left you [behind] in Crete, that you might set right what was defective and finish what was left undone, and that you might appoint elders and set them over the churches (assemblies) in every city as I directed you. [These elders should be] men who are of unquestionable integrity and are irreproachable, the husband of [but] one wife, whose children are [well trained and are] believers, not open to the accusation of being loose in morals and conduct or unruly and disorderly. For the bishop (an overseer) as God's steward must be blameless, not self-willed or arrogant or presumptuous; he must not be

quick-tempered or given to drink or pugnacious (brawling,
violent); he must not be grasping and greedy for filthy lucre
(financial gain); But he must be hospitable (loving and a
friend to believers, especially to strangers and foreigners);
[he must be] a lover of goodness [of good people and good
things], sober-minded (sensible, discreet), upright and fair-
minded, a devout man and religiously correct, temperate
and keeping himself in hand. He must hold fast to the
sure and trustworthy Word of God as he was taught it, so
that he may be able both to give stimulating instruction
and encouragement in sound (wholesome) doctrine and
to refute and convict those who contradict and oppose it
[showing the wayward their error].

The teaching on the Five-Fold Ministry focuses on the character that is required to sustain the ministry and its vision. As a member of the body of Christ, it is necessary to allow the apostolic and prophetic to fine-tune your character to be able to shoulder greater responsibility and accountability. You know, accountability doesn't happen without correction. But, the majority of people in the ministry don't want to be corrected. So, in this chapter, we shall examine the responsibility of the Pastor as the one who corrects and nurtures the babe in the Lord to full maturity in Jesus Christ.

Did you notice in 1 Timothy, Apostle Paul refers to the pastors as overseers (*episcopos* in the Greek), and in Titus, he refers to them as elders (*presbuteros* in Greek)? From this, it can be concluded that there is one office with two different designations. The word "overseer" emphasizes the responsibility of the officeholder to watch over the congregation and meet their spiritual needs, while the word "elder" refers to the life experience of the officeholder.

The Pastor Prepares God's People

The Apostle Paul tells us further what the purpose of the five-fold ministry is. It is to prepare God's people for works of service, *"so that the body of Christ may be built up until we all reach unity in the faith and in the knowledge of the Son of God and become mature, attaining to the whole measure of the fullness of Christ"* (Ephesians 4:12-13 NIV). Since the present body of Christ has definitely not attained the unity in the faith and or the whole measure of the fullness of Christ, the fivefold offices and especially the office of the Pastor are still highly relevant to the body. In fact, judging from the contemporary church and society, the office of the Pastor and the other four offices are needed more than ever before. Therefore the vision of Ephesians 4:12-13 must be fulfilled.

The Pastor's Relationship

Pastors stand in between the demonic Powers and Principalities and their church family in much the same way a father covers his natural family. Because of the close relationship Pastors have with the individual sheep, they are the best equipped to keep the umbrella over the sheep on a one-on-one basis. This is a different umbrella than the apostolic and prophetic covering that is over the entire leadership as well as the flock. In fact, the offices of the Apostle and the Prophet unite to form an umbrella over the entire Universal Church. The Pastor Guards: these are the Feet leading the sheep to rich pasture and paths of righteousness. Their work is continuous, and thus the Pastors are always close by in the life of a believer, providing guidance through all of life's challenges.

The Pastor's Responsibility - The Ring Finger on the Hand of God

The Pastor's office is represented by the ring finger on the Hand of God. This signifies marriage. He is married to the church and must be on the job 24 hours a day. His main function is to love and care for the sheep. It is he who pulls the wool apart to look for spiritual scratches and cuts which go unnoticed many times by the other offices. He displays the unconditional love that God has for His people. No matter how unpleasant the sheep are, the Pastor will always come to their defense.

They are the part of the body of Jesus Christ that knows every hair on your head (Matthew 10:30). The Pastor receives the revelation for the flock and brings it to the house. He talks about the vision, brings the vision to the congregation, and trains them to run with it. He leads them from dry valleys to green pastures. If they fall, he lifts them up. Every time a house member is in need, he is there to bring the love and comfort of God. The Pastor keeps a record of his sheep, and makes sure they are all doing well. He numbers the sheep and notes who is regular at services and who is missing. He is passionate about the congregation he oversees.

The Pastor is the one that has the authority to look after the sheep of his pasture (Psalm 95:7; Psalm 100:3). The pasture belongs to God but God places the Pastor there to care for the sheep on His behalf. Like the caring shepherd, who anoints the sheep against insects (flies and fleas), the Pastor anoints the flock with anointing oil against the attacks of Satan and for their healing (James 5:14).

The Pastor is the one that babysits the new converts brought into the house by the Evangelist (the rescue team). He feeds them with the milk of the word of God. He also discerns the type of word the congregation need at every point in time. As a member of the house, there is a need to desire the sincere milk of the word of God by which you must grow. And so the Pastor determines and decides on the nutritional value of the flock's diet. Only the Pastor can make you hunger and thirst for the word.

> ...as newborn babes, desire the pure milk of the word, that you may grow thereby, if indeed you have tasted that the Lord is gracious (1 Peter 2:2 NKJV).

The Danger of Not Feeding the Sheep

Ezekiel 34:10-15 describes God's response to the shepherds (pastors) who do not feed the sheep (congregation) and allow the sheep to wander about looking for sustenance. Ezekiel warns that God "is against them and will require His flock at their hands." Can you see that the Pastor will be held accountable for the welfare of the congregation? Can you see the seriousness of the Pastor's office? Ezekiel chapters 34, 35, and 36 reveal the heart of God and His displeasure with the shepherds who do not look after the flock.

The Peter Example

> ### John 21:15-17 AMPC
> When they had eaten, Jesus said to Simon Peter, Simon, son of John, do you love Me more than these [others do— with reasoning, intentional, spiritual devotion, as one loves the Father]? He said to Him, Yes, Lord, You know that I love You [that I have deep, instinctive, personal affection for You, as for a close friend]. He said to him, Feed My lambs. Again He said to him the second time, Simon,

son of John, do you love Me [with reasoning, intentional, spiritual devotion, as one loves the Father]? He said to Him, Yes, Lord, You know that I love You [that I have a deep, instinctive, personal affection for You, as for a close friend]. He said to him, Shepherd (tend) My sheep. He said to him the third time, Simon, son of John, do you love Me [with a deep, instinctive, personal affection for Me, as for a close friend]? Peter was grieved (was saddened and hurt) that He should ask him the third time, Do you love Me? And he said to Him, Lord, You know everything; You know that I love You [that I have a deep, instinctive, personal affection for You, as for a close friend]. Jesus said to him, Feed My sheep.

Peter was the first institutional Pastor of the church. He was specifically told by Jesus Christ to feed His sheep, the congregation. The office of the Pastor is so sensitive that Satan wanted to take Peter out, so the flock could be scattered. Remember how Jesus Christ said when the shepherd is attacked, the flock become disoriented and run without any direction and care (Zechariah 13:7; Matthew 26:31)?

In the above conversation with Peter, Jesus Christ specifically handed the office of the Pastor, in which He functioned throughout His ministry on earth, to Peter. However, after the death and resurrection of Jesus Christ, Peter and his team went back to their fishing business as seen in John 21:1-4. When you study these scriptures, you will understand why Jesus Christ had to call upon Peter three times to ask him to feed His sheep. Recognize Jesus Christ confirming Ezekiel's prophecy about the flock and the shepherd (Ezekiel 34:10-15), for the flock belongs to

God) as proven by these scriptures. He is the owner of the house, not the pastors or overseer. This calls for serious accountability and responsibility.

Spiritual Growth and Maturity

Babes in Christ require the milk of the word, but when they grow up they need more solid food.

Hebrews 5:12-14 AMPC

For even though by this time you ought to be teaching others, you actually need someone to teach you over again the very first principles of God's Word. You have come to need milk, not solid food. For everyone who continues to feed on milk is obviously inexperienced and unskilled in the doctrine of righteousness (of conformity to the divine will in purpose, thought, and action), for he is a mere infant [not able to talk yet]! But solid food is for full-grown men, for those whose senses and mental faculties are trained by practice to discriminate and distinguish between what is morally good and noble and what is evil and contrary either to divine or human law.

Hebrews 6:1-3 KJV

Therefore leaving the principles of the doctrine of Christ, let us go on unto perfection; not laying again the foundation of repentance from dead works, and of faith toward God, Of the doctrine of baptisms, and of laying on of hands, and of resurrection of the dead, and of eternal judgment. And this will we do, if God permit.

The Pastor makes sure the congregation is moving towards perfection. He is there on behalf of Jesus Christ the first shepherd and high priest of our calling (Hebrews 4:14-16). Like Jesus Christ, the Pastor loves the church and makes himself available for them, so that the congregation might be sanctified and cleansed by the teaching of the word.

The Pastor also sees that the church is presented a glorious church, not having spot or wrinkle or any such thing, but that she should be holy and without blemish. (Ephesians 5:25-27). It is the responsibility of the Pastor to make sure the congregation is sanctified and cleansed by the word and the vision he brings to them. Like the washing by the water, the teaching of the word is the cleansing process the shepherds take the flock through. Jesus the Chief Pastor and High Priest set the standard when He said you are already clean because of the word which He has spoken to us in John 15:3.

The Pastor Intercedes for the Congregation

Just as Jesus is the ultimate High Priest interceding for us, the Pastor represents Him in a tangible way on earth.

> **Hebrews 7:25 AMPC**
> *Therefore He is able also to save to the uttermost (completely, perfectly, finally, and for all time and eternity) those who come to God through Him, since He is always living to make petition to God and intercede with Him and intervene for them.*

While Jesus Christ is in heaven advocating for us (1 John 2:1-3), the Pastor is here with the church always in the presence of God pleading on behalf of the congregation. Moses, while he was the shepherd leading God's people in the wilderness, set the perfect example of the heart, passion, and the spirit of the pastor. He was always interceding for the people of Israel; even when God wanted to destroy them, Moses stood in the gap (Exodus 32:11-14).

In the same way, the Pastor intercedes for the congregation when they sin. Not only the congregation, but the nation. Let us see how the scriptures explain this is the book of Joel.

> **Joel 2:17 AMPC**
> *Let the priests, the ministers of the Lord, weep between the porch and the altar; and let them say, Have pity and spare Your people, O Lord, and give not Your heritage to reproach, that the [heathen] nations should rule over them or use a byword against them. Why should they say among the peoples, Where is their God?*

From the first line, you see the reference to the "porch" and "altar." That is the Pastor standing in the gap. Whereas the altar in this usage is the place of holiness and forgiveness, the porch demarcates the altar from the pew where the people congregate. The Pastor intercedes for the congregation in love, not condemnation. God is love, and the Pastor is the symbol of God's love and patience towards the body of Christ: the church. The Pastor loves the congregation just as Jesus Christ loves us and gave His life for us. The Pastor is the one in the Five-Fold Ministry that always lays down his life for the congregation.

The Pastor Leads the Congregation in Prayer

A praying pastor will raise up a praying church. He will teach them how to pray through the leading of the Holy Spirit.

> **Romans 8:24-28 AMPC**
>
> *For in [this] hope we were saved. But hope [the object of] which is seen is not hope. For how can one hope for what he already sees? But if we hope for what is still unseen by us, we wait for it with patience and composure. So too the [Holy] Spirit comes to our aid and bears us up in our weakness; for we do not know what prayer to offer nor how to offer it worthily as we ought, but the Spirit Himself goes to meet our supplication and pleads in our behalf with unspeakable yearnings and groanings too deep for utterance. And He Who searches the hearts of men knows what is in the mind of the [Holy] Spirit [what His intent is], because the Spirit intercedes and pleads [before God] in behalf of the saints according to and in harmony with God's will. We are assured and know that [God being a partner in their labor] all things work together and are [fitting into a plan] for good to and for those who love God and are called according to [His] design and purpose.*

These scriptures show the role of the Holy Spirit in equipping the Christian believer in their prayer life. One of the responsibilities of the Pastor is to teach the congregation how to pray just as Jesus Christ taught His disciples how to pray (Matthew 6:5-15). The Holy Spirit brings revelation about the congregation's needs through the word of knowledge. As a result, when the Pastor is praying without being told the problems, he is able to discern the condition of the people through the leading of the Holy Spirit.

Even while we pray, the Holy Spirit comes to our aid to help our prayer life and show us how to pray effectively. An effective prayer life commands the activities in our surroundings to line up with God's plans. Jesus Christ's prayer life was awesome and exceptional such that when the demons saw Him they were petrified.

The Pastor Exemplifies Forgiveness

The Pastor embodies the forgiving nature of Christ. He does not keep a record of the offences of the congregation. Neither does he treat anyone as a sinner because Jesus Christ has already paid the price for sin. Accordingly, what we have is the ministry of reconciliation (2 Corinthians 5:16-21) and not of condemnation (Luke 9:56; John 3:17-21). This is an invitation to enjoy the full purchase of the divine package the Lord Jesus Christ has given us. For, when we were yet sinners, God was in Jesus Christ reconciling the world to Him (Romans 5:6-11). Now let us look at the scriptures for the expression of the love of God.

> ### 1st John 4:16-18 AMPC
> *And we know (understand, recognize, are conscious of, by observation and by experience) and believe (adhere to and put faith in and rely on) the love God cherishes for us. God is love, and he who dwells and continues in love dwells and continues in God, and God dwells and continues in him. In this [union and communion with Him] love is brought to completion and attains perfection with us, that we may have confidence for the day of judgment [with assurance*

and boldness to face Him], because as He is, so are we in this world. There is no fear in love [dread does not exist], but full-grown (complete, perfect) love turns fear out of doors and expels every trace of terror! For fear brings with it the thought of punishment, and [so] he who is afraid has not reached the full maturity of love [is not yet grown into love's complete perfection].

The Pastor Seeks Out the Lost Sheep (Luke 15:1-7)

The Pastor, like the Father and Jesus Christ, searches for the lost. He does not discriminate. He walks in the spirit and not the flesh. He does not recognize the sinner by their sins but sees them through the blood of Jesus Christ. The Pastor receives sinners like Jesus Christ, and cleanses and presents them to God. When members of the congregation are lost, he looks for them. He cares for the church, which is the body of Christ. His joy is in the spiritual development of the congregation.

Compelled by the revelation and the vision, the Pastor and the Evangelist are like scavengers, going through nooks and crannies wherever they can find a soul for the kingdom. With the help of the Holy Spirit, they form the church's divine rescue teams (spiritual first aiders), restoring and resuscitating those who are out of spiritual breath. As God did to Adam (Genesis 2:7), the Pastor breathes the breath of life: hope, reassurance, and confidence into the lost soul to revive them.

Hold Fast the Profession of your Faith – You Are No Longer What You Used To Be

All these heavy responsibilities may look overwhelming for a young or aspiring Pastor. But be assured that you are not doing this in your own strength. You can only do it by the power of the Holy Spirit, who empowers you to function in this office.

> **2 Corinthians 5:14-16 AMPC**
>
> *For the love of Christ controls and urges and impels us, because we are of the opinion and conviction that [if] One died for all, then all died; And He died for all, so that all those who live might live no longer to and for themselves, but to and for Him Who died and was raised again for their sake. Consequently, from now on we estimate and regard no one from a [purely] human point of view [in terms of natural standards of value]. [No] even though we once did estimate Christ from a human viewpoint and as a man...*

You are no longer who you used to be. For if you are in Christ, you are a new creature: old things are passed away; behold all things have become new (2 Corinthians 5:17). So, see yourself as the image and likeness of God (Genesis 1:26-29), which you now are in Christ Jesus. Quit looking down on yourself. In the new creation, it is irrelevant where you came from, what you have been through, and what your inadequacies are. What matters is the revelation, the vision, and the character you now identify with.

The right perception of who you are and how God sees you is essential in functioning in the office of the Pastor. You are not a pastor because you preach every Sunday. You are not a pastor because you stand at the podium. Neither are you a pastor because you wear some kind of robe and pray at the altar. Since the veil of the temple was ripped and torn in two from top to bottom (Mark 15:38; 2 Corinthians 3:12-18), every Christian believer has access to the holy of holies. For all the congregation *"with unveiled face, beholding as in a mirror the glory of the Lord, are being transformed into the same image from glory to glory, just as by the Spirit of the Lord"* (2 Corinthians 3:18 NKJV).

Can you see who you are and how God sees you? Can you see why the office of the Pastor is critical to the transforming of the saints? Beloved, as we close this chapter on the office of the Pastor, recognize that you are what God says you are: a child of the most High (Psalm 82:6). Recognize you are the Pastor bringing the people of God into the knowledge of the revelation and the vision, to the full maturity of the saints in Jesus Christ (Ephesians 4:12-16).

Now let us close this chapter with the following awesome scriptures.

Hebrews 4:16 AMPC

Let us then fearlessly and confidently and boldly draw near to the throne of grace (the throne of God's unmerited favor to us sinners), that we may receive mercy [for our failures] and find grace to help in good time for every need [appropriate help and well-timed help, coming just when we need it].

Hebrews 10:19-21 AMPC

Therefore, brethren, since we have full freedom and confidence to enter into the [Holy of] Holies [by the power and virtue] in the blood of Jesus, By this fresh (new) and living way which He initiated and dedicated and opened for us through the separating curtain (veil of the Holy of Holies), that is, through His flesh, And since we have [such] a great and wonderful and noble Priest [Who rules] over the house of God...

CHAPTER 3

THE EVANGELIST - THE DINNER BELL

Then Jesus went about all the cities and villages, teaching in their synagogues, preaching the gospel of the kingdom, and healing every sickness and every disease among the people. But when He saw the multitudes, He was moved with compassion for them, because they were weary and scattered, like sheep having no shepherd. Then He said to His disciples, "The harvest truly is plentiful, but the laborers are few. Therefore pray the Lord of the harvest to send out laborers into His harvest"

—Matthew 9:35-38 NKJV

Who is the Evangelist?

The Evangelist is a preacher of the Gospel of Jesus Christ, a proclaimer of the good news of salvation in Jesus Christ. Whether he speaks to crowds or on a one-on-one basis, he has the same burning desire to present Jesus Christ to anyone who will listen. And he will be glad to teach you to do the same.

Significance of the Evangelist

Churches need Evangelists, for the harvest is truly plentiful and the laborers are few. Also, understand from Matthew 9:35-38, the office of the Evangelist is about you. Now, I am going to walk you through the scriptures to reveal yourself to you, through talking about you. As a result, you will better understand the purpose, function, and power of the office of the Evangelist.

Remember, the 5-Finger illustration in the introduction? The Middle finger represents the Evangelist: it is the furthest reaching, suggesting its worldwide outreach. There is no limit to the coverage since he is equipped by the Holy Spirit to preach as it were to the uttermost ends of the earth (Acts 1:8). That means the most remote countries in the world.

The 5G Ministry

Let's recap on the five-fold:

The Apostle "Governs" the house (church).

The Prophet "Guides" the house (church).

The Teacher "Grounds" the house (church) in the knowledge of God.

The Evangelist "Gathers" into the house (church).

The Pastors "Guards" the house (church).

Under the 5G Ministry, The Evangelist "Gathers" by training workers or witnesses in how to reach out to the community. The Evangelist both gathers and sows seeds. Not only that, did you observe from the above list that every other ministry ministers to the house (church)? Only the Evangelist gathers **for** the house. You will generally find them outside the house, gathering or reaping the harvest for the house.

(Matthew 9:35-38). Evangelists are reapers or harvesters; they reap or harvest souls. They are kingdom scavengers looking for souls everywhere, anywhere, and this includes slums; anywhere the lost and distressed are found.

Here are some scriptures I have listed for the purpose of this teaching; let's start by reading these scriptures:

> **Proverb 16:1-3 AMP**
>
> *The plans and reflections of the heart belong to man, But the [wise] answer of the tongue is from the Lord. All the ways of a man are clean and innocent in his own eyes [and he may see nothing wrong with his actions], But the Lord weighs and examines the motives and intents [of the heart and knows the truth]. Commit your works to the Lord [submit and trust them to Him], And your plans will succeed [if you respond to His will and guidance].*
>
> **Proverb 16:7 AMP**
>
> *When a man's ways please the LORD, He makes even his enemies to be at peace with him.*

The fivefold creates opportunities for the world to access salvation. Remember the gospel is all about reconciliation and peace (Ephesians 6:15; 2 Corinthians 5:18). As a result, when you please God in doing your part in the fivefold, God moves ahead of you, touching and melting the hearts of those around, as they see in you the light of God's word. You become the beacon of hope, salvation, and reassurance. They will no longer hate you, but accept and love you. This is so profound because the Holy Spirit works in them to draw them closer to the revelation and the vision through you. You are so vital in the vision, to the extent that, if you are not doing your part, the house suffers a loss.

Philippians 2:13 AMP

For it is [not your strength, but it is] God who is effectively at work in you, both to will and to work [that is, strengthening, energizing, and creating in you the longing and the ability to fulfill your purpose] for His good pleasure.

It is therefore crucial to understand in this vision that you are equipped by the Holy Spirit. Armed with the word of God, His revelation and vision, the Holy Spirit will always move with you wherever you need to go. Jesus Christ our Chief Evangelist and Apostle is still working in the house, moving with the fivefold, confirming His word with signs, miracles and wonders (Matthew 28:20; Mark 16:20).

You may think you cannot find the strength and energy when you are out there in the field. But know this: it is when you are doing the work that His strength is manifested in your weakness. You won'te be weak, uneducated, or unskilled in the fivefold. This is because you are invited to come just the way you are, believing and trusting in the power of God.

Think of it this way. If you cannot trust God to the point where He begins to use you to show His love, how do you expect that somebody will believe what you are telling them? So, it begins with you convinced that the Lord, who has sent you, is able to accomplish His vision and purpose in you and through you.

It is crucial to walk in the evangelistic office that Jesus Christ walked in because, if you don't walk as Christ did, you will be missing the most exciting ministry in the body of Christ. It is so exciting because it is part of the new creation. It wasn't exposed in the Old Testament because then it was not required. Consequently, there were no Evangelists in the Old Testament. Jesus Christ, whose purpose was evangelism had already been revealed by the Prophets of the Old Testament; although He had not yet physically manifested and suffered crucifixion. So, the evangelistic office that Jesus Christ functioned in was something totally new.

There was always the office of Apostle, the Prophet, the Teacher, and Pastor. But, the office of the Evangelist had not been experienced before. When Jesus Christ came with the office of the Evangelist in the New Testament, it took people by surprise. The office of the Evangelist heralded the new creation. Jesus Christ through the office of the Evangelist started all over the business of creation that God had completed in the Old Testament (Genesis 1 and 2). But here was the exception. The new creation Jesus Christ was creating was unique in that He equipped His new creation to **recreate** just as He did. In the old creation, Adam, though he had the image and likeness of God (Genesis 1:26-27) only had dominion over creation (Genesis 1:28), but he was not empowered to create and recreate like God.

However, in the new creation, the new Adam, the church of the firstborn, He was empowered not only to have dominion over creation but to create and recreate like God. I am not saying we have the ability to create physical life, but we have the same ability (the Holy Spirit and the Word) like God and Jesus Christ to lead people to the rebirth. Hence, in the new creation through the operation of the spoken word, the Evangelist can raise the dead, heal the sick, recreate a broken tissue, and fix a broken bone, by the same Holy Spirit that operated in Jesus Christ (Romans 8:11-14).

Recall how Adam and Eve through the seduction of Satan messed everything up in the old creation (Genesis 3). Jesus Christ in the new creation came to set things in order. He came with a worldwide vision confirmed in (Acts 1:8) that saw the new creature through salvation exported to every nation of the world by the office of the Evangelist. The office of the Evangelist is so significant and strategic in the new creation because it first reveals you to you. It then empowers you to know who you are, what your weaknesses are, and how to handle them. Adam and Eve, though blessed, another word to mean "empowered," didn't understand the magnitude of their office as the first creation.

They did not understand their godly nature in that they had been empowered to be like God and to dominate the earth. Satan had manipulated them to think they needed to strive to be what they already were. However, they had to work through their own faith as they didn't have the revelation and energizing of the Holy Spirit.

Looking at the scriptures again from the AMPC version, let's recite this awesome scripture:

> Not in your own strength for it is God Who is all the while effectually at work in you energizing and creating in you the power and desire, both to will and to work for His good pleasure and satisfaction and delight (Philippians 2:13).

The above scripture refers to you, who have the new nature. Appropriating it for yourself will make a remarkable difference between what you were and what you are in the new creation.

The Father's Dinner Bell of Love

Now, here is the word that the Lord gave me when I was preparing this teaching.

I'm my Father's Dinner Bell of Love. I'm a picture of the Heart of a Father, who is the Creator of His children. I'm an instrument of Love. My love and my faith causes others to receive the manifestation of my Father's will. I demonstrated His Love by Miracles, Signs, and Wonders. The Father's will has always been for His creation to be whole. He created them whole so that by His Love and with miracles, signs and wonders, the Father, through me, would manifest His love now.

Here's the word of the Lord for the Evangelist:

> *"The time has come for you to be the instrument of love to My creation and bring them back to Me now. O the time is right, and I am ready to work with you like never before. I have saved the best for now. Not only miracles, signs, and wonders, but the New Birth and Sonship. I want to work with you to bring my sons and daughters back to Me. Will you be My Dinner Bell now? Work with Me now, and I will show through you what My Love is for My creation. Come and join Me and, we will get them back*
>
> *Jesus' first miracle was in a place where there was a want, not a need. The people you will be coming into contact with also want to be healed, and you are the instrument the Father will use with the help of The Holy Spirit. You won't be concerned about sin though, since you recognize that sin has been paid for by Jesus. They don't.*
>
> *There will be those who will need a miracle, and the Holy Spirit will work through you by giving you simple*

instructions. Remember, Jesus was always teaching about the Kingdom and demonstrating its power. Now it's your time to do the same with the help of the Holy Ghost.

Remember, too, that everyone connected to Jesus and everyone connected to those who are connected to Jesus Christ could receive from Jesus. As you step out in Love, that makes faith work in you and through you. Lives will be changed because you are My Dinner Bell now. Let's Go And Get The Job Done!!!!!"

Can you see that? Isn't that awesome? What amazing grace and love! Now, I want to walk you through some scriptures, starting from Genesis 1. God never changes His mind. If you find out what was on God's mind, in the beginning, you will have an idea why the office of Evangelist is so important.

Genesis 1:26-28 AMP

Then God said, "Let Us (Father, Son, Holy Spirit) make man in Our image, according to Our likeness [not physical, but a spiritual personality and moral likeness]. (Make new beginnings. Make you in them in my image and my likeness, to look like me and acts like me). And let them have complete authority over the fish of the sea, the birds of the air, the cattle, and over the entire earth, and over everything that creeps and crawls on the earth."

So God created man in His own image, in the image and likeness of God He created him; male and female He created them. And God blessed them and said to them, Be fruitful, multiply, and fill the earth, and subdue it [using

all its vast resources in the service of God and man]; and
have dominion over the fish of the sea, the birds of the air,
and over every living creature that moves upon the earth.

Verse 28 has the secret: God blessed and empowered them. When you look at the evangelistic office you really start to think of being blessed or empowered. The evangelistic office is the most exciting office because, to function in it, you have to understand your need to go into the office not thinking about sin or sinners.

Remember, the Apostle Paul talked about being transformed and renewed in our mind (Romans 12:2). Yes, you need a changed or a transformed mindset, not dwelling on sin to function in the evangelistic office. You really cannot function in this office if you are judgmental and critical of sinners. Or go out looking for sin or sinners.

If you go out on the street looking for sinners, you will find them in abundance because Satan has turned the world into a slum, and you know what you get in a shanty town. Jesus Christ put it this way, "*I send you out as sheep in the midst of wolves*" (Matthew 10:16).

Likewise, if you go out there saying you want to get someone saved, and you judged them by the flesh (flesh in this usage means by their character, behavior, or manner) you are going to walk away empty-handed. You cannot have Jesus' heart as an Evangelist and be judgmental or critical. It makes sense that you can't be the accuser and at the same time be the solution. As Chief Evangelist Jesus Christ was also the Chief Prophet, Chief Apostle, Chief Shepherd and Chief Teacher. He didn't become part of the problem of the sinner; He became the solution.

You can't judge them by their flesh but by the heart of Jesus and His heart is, "I am your Helper."

> *My dear children, I write this letter to you so you will not sin. But if anyone does sin, we have a helper in the presence of the Father—Jesus Christ, the One who does what is right. He died in our place to take away our sins, and not only our sins but the sins of all people (1 John 2:1-2 NCV).*

Power of the Evangelistic Office

Can you see the office of the Evangelist is also about your perception, revealing who you are? Can you see why you cannot continue doing what you have been doing before? Let me show you how powerful the evangelistic office is. The evangelistic office is the office where the gifts of the Holy Spirit flow in abundant measure with miracles, signs, and wonders. When you come across a soul in need of your ministration, the anointing in you influences the environment and the soul, making it easier for the Word of God to come through. As you continue in your ministration the Lord through the Word of knowledge reveals to you the name of the person, the problem, or what want or desire. This was the case with the Samaritan woman who Jesus Christ met at Jacob's well (John 4:1-25).

Now, you will observe the Holy Spirit introducing you to all of the gifts that flow in the office of the Evangelist. An essential gift that is distinctive in the evangelistic office is the word of knowledge. (1 Corinthians 12:8).

For instance, you go out to speak to somebody about the new creation. Before you meet the person, God has already given you the name of that person and a word for them. Now you are vigilant and sensitive enough to the Spirit to identify the right person. Then, the Holy Spirit prompts you to reach out to that particular person. You step out in the faith, boldness, and confidence of the Holy Spirit by greeting the person and conveying the message the Lord gave you. This person does not even know you; nor are you acquainted with the person.

However, the accuracy and timeliness of the word will compel the person to give you an audience. The gifts, especially in the evangelistic office on the street, are amazing. Remember Philip the Evangelist and the Ethiopian Eunuch (Acts 8:26-40)? But some people will discern something and judge it to be wrong because they lack an accurate understanding of the special anointing of the Evangelist. The scriptures call this the zeal of the Lord, but not according to human knowledge (Romans 10:2-4). If you don't understand the Lord's mind concerning the new beginning, the flesh will distract you. So, three essential characteristics of the word of knowledge are that it is specific, accurate, and timely (SAT).

The Model of an Evangelist

Jesus Christ is the Bible's best model of an Evangelist. He taught the disciples and the new creation (the church) how to fish for souls by demonstrating the power of God through miracles, signs, and wonders. Jesus Christ's prayer life was so amazing because, as soon as He was through with His prayers, He was fired-up. The people were drawn to Him and started following Him. Jesus Christ was an apostolic preacher, who also operated in the office of the Evangelist. What does the Evangelist do? He stands in the gap. The whole essence of evangelism is helping God's creation to know Him. Let's turn to our Bibles now:

> ### Luke 4:18 AMPC
> *The Spirit of the Lord [is] upon Me, because He has anointed Me [the Anointed One, the Messiah] to preach the good news (the Gospel) to the poor; He has sent Me to announce release to the captives and recovery of sight to the blind, to send forth as delivered those who are oppressed [who are downtrodden, bruised, crushed, and broken down by calamity] . . .*

> ### 2 Corinthians 8:9 AMPC
> *For you are becoming progressively acquainted with and recognizing more strongly and clearly the grace of our Lord Jesus Christ (His kindness, His gracious generosity, His undeserved favor and spiritual blessing), [in] that though He was [so very] rich, yet for your sakes He became [so very] poor, in order that by His poverty you might become enriched (abundantly supplied).*

As an Evangelist, taking your cue from the above scriptures, you both have and are the good news for the poor. Jesus paid the price for you not to be poor, and for the folks out there on the street not to be poor either. Evangelism is telling the poor they have been liberated from poverty, material and spiritual poverty.

Would you mind telling somebody that?

Just as Jesus Christ was the Chief Evangelist in looking for disciples, one of the responsibilities of the Evangelist is to look for disciples. Jesus Christ described evangelism as fishing for souls (making disciples) in the ocean of mankind. "*I will make you fishers of men*" (Matthew 4:19) and (Luke 5:10), Jesus Christ caught His fish (people) by telling them the good news and confirming it with miracles, signs, and wonders (Mark 16:20).

In short, you have to see yourself as God planned you to be. In the office of the Evangelist, you are anointed with the Holy Spirit and with power (Acts 10:38).

THE CHARACTER OF THE
FIVE-FOLD MINISTRY

LOVE

Through the Lens of

CHAPTER FOUR

THE PROPHET - GOD'S EYES AND VOICE

1 Corinthians 12:28 AMP

So God has appointed and placed in the church [for His own use]: first apostles [chosen by Christ], second prophets [those who foretell the future, those who speak a new message from god to the people], third teachers, then those who work miracles, then those with the gifts of healings, the helpers, the administrators, and speakers in various kinds of [unknown] tongues.

"Now it's Time for My Eyes and Voice to go to the Corporate Level."

Genesis 11:6 AMPC

And the Lord said, Behold, they are one people and they have all one language; and this is only the beginning of what they will do, and now nothing they have imagined they can do will be impossible for them.

The Word of the Lord to His Prophets

"I have given you My eyes and My tongue. Now the time has come for you to give them back to Me so that I may

show you how to see and speak like Me in a new and fresh way. My time has come to show Myself strong through my whole body. The time has also come for you to show forth how it was always supposed to be. There are more dimensions in Me than anyone has ever seen or heard. I am so diversified that it will amaze even you. So now give Me back what I gave you and watch Me use you as I have always planned to.

Be all that I want you to be and to do. I have chosen you for a time like this (John 15:16). A time is coming that has never been before; when I am about to pour out My Spirit on all flesh (Joel 2:28; Acts 2:17-18) so that I can show My Love for My creation like never before.

Come and give so that you can receive like never before. Turn around and release my anointing from your new dimension."

One of the key goals of the Prophet's office is bringing the disciples of Jesus Christ to the place where they begin to manifest as in Genesis 11:6. His anointing creates unity in the vision. Everyone knows the vision and everyone also knows the revelation that there will come a time that you will receive the invitation to be a part of the vision. How awesome it will it be when everyone knows the vision and comes together in the unity and the understanding that embraces the vision!

Who Is The Prophet?

The Prophet is the one who lays the foundation of the vision and recognizes that the vision is always about redemption. Everybody's dream is connected to the vision and the vision is about being in the right place at the right time. One thing we have always done in the ministry is to encourage people to be where they are supposed to be. As a result, the Lord will place you in the pasture where you are going to be fed (Psalm 23).

Often, however, the majority of people get frustrated in their community church, not because the church isn't good but, because the Lord didn't put them there – they picked the place. They decided on the church based on their preferences rather than allowing the Lord to direct them. As they are not properly fed, they get frustrated.

Nine times out of ten, the Lord is going to put you in a place (pasture or church) that is going to benefit you the most. If the place the Lord has prepared for you is going to benefit you the most, it also means it is going to challenge you the most. In the house where God chooses to bless you, you will always be challenged to be your best. The whole purpose for the apostolic and the prophetic offices is to bring you to a place where you surrender and allow God to groom you just as the Vinedresser grooms the vine (John 15:1-8).

The Duties Of The Prophet

> *I Corinthians 12:6-7 AMP*
> *And there are [distinctive] ways of working [to accomplish things], but it is the same God who produces all things in all believers [inspiring, energizing, and empowering them]. But to each one is given the manifestation of the Spirit [the spiritual illumination and the enabling of the Holy Spirit] for the common good.*

The Prophet Guides

He is like the mouth, communicating guidance. He takes his words from God and reveals this to the congregation.

Going back to the finger of God illustration The Forefinger represents the Prophet. Its purpose is to point towards a certain direction. The function of pointing is not just to show direction, but so that it can be followed by an action. This action is the one that guides believers in the same direction in which the "finger" is pointing. In addition, the Prophets are problem solvers. They find the solution to any problem at the place of intercession as they seek the face of God.

The Prophet's first duty is to teach the vision, train, activate, and impart the anointing to prophesy. While the anointing on the Prophet can be transferred, the office cannot. This transferred anointing gives the receiver the same ability to edify, exhort, and comfort, and opens the door for everyone to be evangelistic. There is an anointing on the Prophet to be released to those around him to have a greater ability to discern by the leading of the Holy Spirit.

The prophetic revelation of the vision is vital to the prosperity of the disciples. The greater the revelation of the vision, the greater the focus on the vision, the more the dreams of the whole congregation will come to pass, and testimonies will increase. When the Prophet is balanced in his calling, the strength of the congregation is increased. As the scriptures rightly put it, when the foundation is solid, the family can be as large as the Father has planned it to be, yet not lose its togetherness.

Becoming Your Best

Ephesians 4:11-13 AMP

11And [His gifts to the church were varied and] He Himself appointed some as apostles [special messengers, representatives], some as prophets [who speak a new message from God to the people], some as evangelists [who spread the good news of salvation], and some as pastors and teachers [to shepherd and guide and instruct], 12[and He did this] to fully equip and perfect the saints (God's people) for works of service, to build up the body of Christ [the church]; 13until we all reach oneness in the faith and in the knowledge of the Son of God, [growing spiritually] to become a mature believer, reaching to the measure of the fullness of Christ [manifesting His spiritual completeness and exercising our spiritual gifts in unity].

The office of the Prophet is to help the believer grow up. Here is the question: can you help children grow up without correcting them? In understanding the vision, you are to be stretched to be your best. When you understand the vision and recognize it is about redemption, then your dream will be accomplished.

For instance, when you work for an employer, your employer owns the vision. You are there to help your employer fulfill the vision and you are paid to do so. Likewise, when you come into the kingdom, your desire is to fulfill His vision because He gave it to you. Remember, the scriptures say, "Seek ye first the kingdom of God and His Righteousness and . . ." (Mathew 6:33)?

Have you ever seen a man who had everything, but didn't have a family? In the real sense, he didn't have everything because he had no family. The world's standard is always about success, individuality, and personal aspirations. But in the kingdom it is the opposite. The kingdom is all about family. Remember, from the creation, it has always been about family. Now let's go into the Word to see what the responsibilities of the Prophets are.

> **1 Corinthians 14:1 AMPC**
> *Eagerly pursue and seek to acquire [this] love [make it your aim, your great quest]; and earnestly desire and cultivate the spiritual endowments (gifts), especially that you may prophesy (interpret the divine will and purpose in inspired preaching and teaching).*

This scripture shows us the responsibilities of the Prophet. Any prophet that does nothing else except to prophecy is not balanced because that is not the focus of the Prophet's office. The focus of the Prophet is to lay the foundation of the vision as it is recorded in the above scriptures.

The Prophet, the Family, and the Vision

> **Numbers 11:26 AMP**
> *But two men had remained in the camp; one named Eldad and the other named Medad. The Spirit rested upon them (now they were among those who had been registered, but had not gone out to the Tent), and they prophesied in the camp.*

The Lord chose His Prophets in the Old Testament. As we discussed earlier, the office of the Prophet and the other offices, except for the office of the Evangelist, have been fully operational since Old Testament times. God always had specific people anointed to operate in the office of the Prophet, and it is still largely so today. The only difference is that we, as the new creation in Christ Jesus, now have the capacity through the Holy Spirit to function in any of the offices as the Spirit leads.

Numbers 11:29 AMP

But Moses said to him, "Are you jealous for my sake? Would that all the Lord's people were prophets and that the Lord would put His Spirit upon them!"

Moses was one of the few leaders in the Old Testament that functioned in several offices as a result of his role in leading the people of God out of Egypt and in the wilderness. Not everyone can be a Prophet as indicated by Moses. The body of believers is made of several unique parts that work in unity for the maturity of the saints (Romans 12:4-6; 1 Corinthians 12:12-27). But, it is also essential to recognize in the New Testament that, though everybody cannot run the same office, still, that potential exists with every member of the house as the Holy Spirit directs. Thus, there can be no jealousy in the body.

1 Corinthians 14:3 AMP

But [on the other hand] the one who prophesies speaks to people for edification [to promote their spiritual growth] and [speaks words of] encouragement [to uphold and advise them concerning the matters of God] and [speaks words of] consolation [to compassionately comfort them].

When the Prophet develops love for the vision, he brings the family into that vision, encouraging them to prophesy in their own words. The Prophet teaches the family that they have an anointing on them to prophesy to people around them from the revelation they have received from the Holy Spirit through the gift of the word of knowledge.

The Lord can give you insight about those around you to encourage, to edify, to exalt, and to build them up until they come to the full maturity of the saints in the light. Can you see the relevance of the Prophet in the house, encouraging the congregation to grow into the vision and the character of Christ?

So, the Prophet in the house encourages the whole house. They get the attention of the congregation, through the insight of the Holy Spirit to get them to the place where the Lord wants them to be. The Prophet understands that anybody in the house can learn how to prophesy and to edify one another.

In the family, the roles of the Pastor and the Prophet converge. As the Prophet, you speak to the spirit and not the flesh. The office of the Prophet is so vital to the five-fold character because you are going to learn how to discern in the spirit and how to bring the right word into any situation.

The Prophet does not look at the flesh but discerns in the spirit. You know it is easy to prophesy about the flesh because you judge the individual by their behavior and not by insight. The Prophet in the house prepares the house to receive from the Holy Spirit. Do you know the Holy Spirit bears witness with your spirit (Romans 8:16) and not with your flesh? Remember the deep calling to the deep (Psalm 42:7)?

The Prophet in the house sees the opportunity, not the job. If you see the task you get frustrated, but when you see the opportunity you are motivated. Thus, the Prophet in the house teaches the house how to discern in the Holy Spirit. The Prophet loves the people enough to pray for individuals with issues, seeking from the Lord what the problems are so they can be helped. The Prophet is the one concerned about the welfare of the house. He always prays for revelation on how to improve the house. He is always seeking insight into how to build the house.

The Prophet has full knowledge of the individual's personality. And he speaks to the individual from the inside out. This is not what he see with his human observation but, from the revelation from the word of knowledge the Lord gives him about the individual in the house. That is why we must walk in love. If you don't walk in love, you will be a critic and prophesy from the flesh. The prophetic office in the body of Christ is the opportunity to edify and to build the church.

However, often the Prophet allows himself to be frustrated with the flesh. As long you are frustrated with the flesh you can never flow with the Holy Spirit, His gifts and the office of the Prophet. This happens because as the prophet of the house he is not balancing prophecy with teaching.

Can you also observe the Prophet as the sent one? God can send a Prophet in the house to bring a message to the congregation or to an individual or a family in the vision. Though He demonstrated this throughout the Old Testament, the Prophet was not of the house. But in the New Testament, the Prophets are in the house.

The Significance of the Prophet's Office

The Prophet in the house saves life and prevents disaster. For instance, in Daniel Chapter 2, King Nebuchadnezzar had dreams. As a result of these dreams, he became anxious and lost his sleep. The king sent for the magicians, the astrologers, the sorcerers, and the Chaldeans to reveal his dreams. This was a new dimension because what these prophets were used to was the interpretation of dreams. They were not trained in finding or knowing the dream first and then bringing the interpretation. So, they approached the king:

> Then said the Chaldeans [diviners] to the king in Aramaic [the Syrian language], O king, live forever! Tell your servants the dream, and we will show the interpretation (Daniel 2:4 AMP).

But the king had no recollection of the dreams. Again, he instructed the magicians to find his dream and its "interpretation." The magicians answered again,

> "There is not a man on earth who can tell the king's matter; therefore no king, lord, or ruler has ever asked such things of any magician, astrologer, or Chaldean. It is a difficult thing that the king requests, and there is no other who can tell it to the king except the gods, whose dwelling is not with flesh" (Daniel 2:10-11 AMP).

They recognized their limitations and claimed that only the gods could meet the demands of the king. Now King Nebuchadnezzar was livid.

> For this cause the king was angry and very furious and commanded that all the wise men of Babylon be destroyed. So the decree went forth that the wise men were to be killed, and [the officers] sought Daniel and his companions to be slain (Daniel 2:12-13 AMP).

The Prophet in the House

Daniel had heard of the king's order and approached the officer in charge of executing the king's order of eliminating the magicians.

> Then Daniel returned an answer which was full of prudence and wisdom to Arioch the captain or executioner of the king's guard, who had gone forth to slay the wise men of Babylon. He said to Arioch, the king's captain, Why is the decree so urgent and hasty from the king? Then Arioch explained the matter to Daniel (Daniel 2:14-15 AMP).

Understand Daniel's steps. They underscore every step required by the Prophet in dealing with a crisis or a negative situation. Daniel requested of the king some time to discern his dream and provide the interpretation; he then went back to his companions to brief them on the development.

> Then Daniel went to his house and made the thing known to Hananiah, Mishael, and Azariah, his companions, So that they would desire and request mercy of the God of heaven concerning this secret, that Daniel and his companions should not perish with the rest of the wise men of Babylon. Then the secret was revealed to Daniel in a vision of the night, and Daniel blessed the God of heaven (Daniel 2:17-19 AMP).

Can you see the Prophet working with his team and flowing with the other offices and gifts? And as they prayed seeking insight from God, God revealed King Nebuchadnezzar's dream and the interpretation to Daniel.

Recognize and Celebrate the Opportunity

Daniel did not run to the king with his dream and the interpretation. He proved to God his priorities by first taking time to worship, praise, and thank God for the vision as seen here:

Daniel answered, Blessed be the name of God forever and ever! For wisdom and might are His! He changes the times and the seasons; He removes kings and sets up kings. He gives wisdom to the wise and knowledge to those who have understanding! He reveals the deep and secret things; He knows what is in the darkness, and the light dwells with Him! I thank You and praise You, O God of my fathers, Who has given me wisdom and might and has made known to me now what we desired of You, for You have made known to us the solution to the king's problem (Daniel 2:20-23 AMP).

It was after Daniel had exalted God in the place of intercessory prayer that he went back to the officer in charge of eliminating the magicians and their team.

A Man with the Solution

Asking the officer in charge to put the killing of the magicians on hold, he requested to be brought before the king. The officer quickly took Daniel to the king.

. . . I have found a man of the captives of Judah who will make known to the king the interpretation [of his dream]. The king said to Daniel, whose name was Belteshazzar, Are

you able to make known to me the dream which I
have seen and interpretation of it? (Daniel 2:25-26
AMPC).

Before the next discussion, let me bring you back to the difference between the job and the opportunity as exemplified by Daniel's response to King Nebuchadnezzar's queries. Daniel saw the opportunity to bring heaven down. He was working with the vision of the house which is to reveal the Father. Daniel never lost an opportunity to glorify God. Can you see the prophetic office is not only about prophesying, but it is also the office where you find solutions to the problems of the house, corporate bodies, and the nation?

Food for Thought

Will you be the Daniel (Prophet) in your, generation? The one that can stand in the gap as the Prophet in the house to provide solutions to family, corporation, and national issues? When the president is urgent need of a solution approaches the church, would you rise to the challenge?

Daniel answered the king, The [mysterious] secret which
the king has demanded neither the wise men, enchanters,
magicians, nor astrologers can show the king, But there is
a God in heaven Who reveals secrets, and He has made
known to King Nebuchadnezzar what it is that shall be in
the latter days (at the end of days). Your dream and the
visions in your head upon your bed are these: As for you, O
king, as you were lying upon your bed thoughts came into
your mind about what should come to pass hereafter, and
He Who reveals secrets was making known to you what

shall come to pass. But as for me, this secret is not revealed to me for any wisdom that I have more than anyone else living, but in order that the interpretation may be made known to the king and that you may know the thoughts of your heart and mind (Daniel 2:27-30 AMPC).

Thus, Daniel revealed the king's dream in (Daniel 2:31-36) and gave the interpretation (Daniel 2:37-45). From now on Daniel and his team had a new status – a promotion (Daniel 2:46-49).

Beloved, can you see the power of the Holy Spirit and the Prophet's office to reveal secrets, save lives, and prevent crises? The understanding of the vision of the prophetic office is crucial for promoting the Father's heart of love of redemption. And the Father is going to give you a new reputation wherever you go, revealing the vision in that situation. Just as King Nebuchadnezzar in Daniel 2 understood Daniel had what he needed, and came to Daniel again for another interpretation (Daniel 4), the family (the congregation) understands you have what they need. When they need help they can always come to you. There is nobody in the house that is not qualified to prophesy and operate in the office and gifts that are required at a specific time. Like Daniel demonstrated, the Prophet works in love and flows in the office and gifts that are necessary at the time. Again, as seen from Daniel, if your prayer life is right, the interpretation can come as a word of knowledge, a word of wisdom, and even the working of miracles (1 Corinthians 12:8).

Be the Solution in Your Occupation and Ministry

Therefore, the person who speaks in an [unknown] tongue should pray [for the power] to interpret and explain what he says (1 Corinthians 14:13 AMPC).

The Prophet prays in the Spirit seeking insight for what is needed. You can do this in your occupation and ministry, praying for solutions to problems. The office of the Prophet is authorized to change and transform destinies. Like Daniel, the Prophet has the capacity to stop disasters. You can prophesy and bring a warning, sometimes to individuals – however, you cannot stop them from making their own choices. Your responsibility is to present the message to the one addressed.

I Corinthians 14:22-25 AMPC

Thus [unknown] tongues are meant for a [supernatural] sign, not for believers but for unbelievers [on the point of believing], while prophecy (inspired preaching and teaching, interpreting the divine will and purpose) is not for unbelievers [on the point of believing] but for believers. Therefore, if the whole church assembles and all of you speak in [unknown] tongues, and the ungifted and uninitiated or unbelievers come in, will they not say that you are demented? But if all prophesy [giving inspired testimony and interpreting the divine will and purpose] and an unbeliever or untaught outsider comes in, he is told of his sin and reproved and convicted and convinced by all, and his defects and needs are examined (estimated, determined) and he is called to account by all, The secrets of his heart are laid bare; and so, falling on [his] face, he will worship God, declaring that God is among you in very truth.

Do you understand those scriptures? The focus is on the outsider being reproved, convicted, and convinced by the house. For better understanding here is an illustration.

You've just got to church and you are prompted by the Holy Spirit to stay outside the building praying in the Holy Spirit (Jude 1:20). Now as you are out there praying, the Lord reveals to you there is going to be a guest in the house today. The Lord gives you the specifics about this guest. The Lord says the guest will drive up in a particular type of car with a specific color and also gives you the color of the shirt he is wearing. The Lord says, "Tell him the Lord has something for him today."

As you continue to pray in the Holy Ghost, a car drives into the church premises and pulls over just as the Lord had told you. As the man steps out of the car, you walk over to this gentleman, welcome him, and say to him, "The Lord has told me about you." You repeat the specifics about the car and perhaps his shirt. Now you have his attention. He walks into the house, takes his seat, and waits for you to tell him what the Lord said about him.

But this time, not you, but another member of the house thats in charge of that section where the gentleman sits is praying in the Holy Ghost about those who will sit on that pew. He meets him and says to him, "The Lord said He was going to do such and such for you. Do you have any confirmation about that? He's dumbstruck at the accuracy in which the word of knowledge is flowing. He will, without a doubt, make up his mind to stay, even if he had planned on walking out of the house when the sermon becomes uninteresting or when he doesn't fancy the preacher's style.

Can you see that? That is what the Prophet does. The Prophet sets the tone for everybody to understand the vision and flow in the offices and the gifts as is required in season. Can you see how important you are in the house? You are all demonstrating corporate and coordinated anointing, because it is not one person, it is the entire house. This is the sum of the prophetic.

Beloved, as we come to the end of this chapter, let's remind ourselves of the need to continually grow together in the unity of the vision and revelation as revealed by Apostle Paul:

> **Ephesians 2:20-21 AMP**
>
> . . . *²⁰having been built on the foundation of the apostles and prophets, with Christ Jesus Himself as the [chief] Cornerstone, ²¹in whom the whole structure is joined together, and it continues [to increase] growing into a holy temple in the Lord [a sanctuary dedicated, set apart, and sacred to the presence of the Lord].*

THE CHARACTER OF THE
FIVE-FOLD MINISTRY

Through the Lens of

LOVE

CHAPTER FIVE

THE APOSTLE – THE FACE OF GOD

"Get Ready! Get Ready! Get Ready!

"Have you ever tasted something and all of your senses began to come alive? Well, get ready to enjoy one of the best adventures of your life as you digest this awesome, fresh and insightful statement of Love from Me your Father describing Myself as the only One who can call Himself the "I AM." Do you know that I AM is all-inclusive. Everything comes in I AM. Take your time and enjoy this delicious meal and watch the Lover of your soul become your everything.

"Your Best Has Just Begun!!!

Love Forever
Dad"

To My Special Messenger: the Apostle

"To my burden-removing, yoke-destroying ambassador; to my personal representative; to my example, to my sample.

"Look at what I have said to you. You are My special messenger. As you understand this one thing, I will always show Myself strong through you. Your time with Me is your key to learning My ways and being in a place where you can trust Me more and more. There are those who will not be great for Me because they will not give me the time with them that I desire to allow Me to develop them to be all that I know they can be. BUT NOT YOU! I have shown you how important your time with me can be. I will make everything easy as you allow Me to work in you so that what I have done in secret the world will be able to enjoy.

"I Love My Creation and I have chosen you to prove My love in very special ways. Life was never meant to be hard; but most of all, My children don't know that yet. So now, I have decided to show Myself strong through My Church, My Body, and My Kingdom. Now I have prepared all things, for now I want to demonstrate what I did when I made the New Creation, the New Creature all together, the fresh and New Creature. Now I have chosen you for this great honor.

"Will you allow Me to show My love to My New Creatures and disciple them into the massive army that cannot be defeated? It's My victory. It's what I have already won. Now I want to display My victory through you. My love will now make My faith work in you and for you and through you for others like never before.

"I am ready. Are you willing to show Me to the world in a fresh new way? Come to Me now so that I can send you as I have already planned. The world is waiting for

Me to come back. Let me come back in you and through you now like never before. The journey will be awesome, wonderful, and magnificent – more than you could have ever imagined.

"I am ready to reveal Myself now, so Let's Get Started!!"

In the teaching of the Five-Fold Ministry Jesus Christ was not talking only about the gift but the character of the fivefold ministers. Most people get thrilled because of the gift. The scriptures say a man's gift makes room for him and brings him before great men (Proverbs 18:16). This is accurate. So, they are not wrong to be excited about the gifts of the fivefold. Besides, most people are excited about the gift because the gifts came first.

However, people can often get carried away by the gifts, and neglect the Fruit that has to do with the character of the fivefold.

That is why what I am going to teach you about the office of the Apostle is so crucial to the vision. This is the vision which you are part of, which you are always praying and standing in the gap for. The office of the Apostle is important because it comes first. The Apostle gets the revelation and brings it to the church. Recognize that the gifts are already there; but character is required to sustain the gift. If, the character is not right, the abuse of the gifts is inevitable.

Often, we observe the contemporary apostles doing things they are not supposed to do. This is a sign of the absence of character in the Gift and in the Vision. What the Apostle is supposed to do is to identify the vision in such an awesome way such that what we read in Ephesians 4:11-13 becomes absolutely and inevitably crucial to the church. Let us start now from the foundation to see exactly what the responsibilities of the Apostles are.

> **Ephesians 4:11-17 AMPC**
>
> *And His gifts were [varied; He Himself appointed and gave men to us]* **(this means to the vision)** *some to be apostles (special messengers), some prophets (inspired preachers and expounders), some evangelists (preachers of the Gospel, traveling missionaries), some pastors (shepherds of His flock) and teachers. His intention was the perfecting and the full equipping of the saints (His consecrated people), [that they should do] the work of ministering toward building up Christ's body (the church)* **(So, what is that all about? It is about maturity, revelation)** *[That it might develop] until we all attain oneness in the faith and in the comprehension of the full and accurate] knowledge of the Son of God, that [we might arrive] at really mature manhood (the completeness of personality which is nothing less than the standard height of Christ's own perfection), the measure of the stature of the fullness of the Christ and the completeness found in Him (emphasis added).*

It is the responsibility of the Apostle to identify the vision as seen in the above scriptures. The church is hindered when they are not mature.

The gifts of Jesus Christ were varied; He appointed and gave men to the vision. His intention was to cause them to grow, to build up the body – the character. The essence of the apostolic is to cause growth and maturity in the revelation. Hence, the Apostle functions in anointing and power.

Do you know that when you understand who you are in the vision, everybody around will be intimidated by your presence? When you discover your personality in the revelation, it is absolutely awesome. You will walk without any trace of fear because you are walking in love. When you walk in love you have no fear because perfect love casts out all fear (1 John 4:18).

When you walk in love, you can't stand the notion of not obeying what the Lord tells you to do. The apostolic brings you to that place of prayer where you can love and trust the Lord enough to do everything He asks you to do. You do so purely out of love for the Lord and it's easy to obey His instructions. The Lord loves you into trusting Him. You know that when you love somebody, it is easy to obey. So, what the apostolic does is to bring you a place where you begin to trust the Lord totally.

I want to show you three key areas about the apostolic. Everybody in the New Testament knew what the Apostle was because the Apostle, unlike the Evangelist, was a familiar figure. Remember, unlike the Evangelist, the Apostle had always been there from Old Testament times.

Note, the predominant occupation of the Israelites was farming (animal farming and agriculture) so the Apostle was associated with looking after the flocks. Like we saw in the office of the Pastor, the Apostle oversees the general church, that is, the flock of Jesus Christ. He has them trained. They are identified as those who would take territories in the name of Jesus Christ. They are always found in the secret place of the Most High (Psalm 91), praying for partnership, pulling down strongholds (2 Corinthians 10:3-5), demonic forces, and the powers of darkness.

> *For though we walk in the flesh, we do not war according to the flesh. For the weapons of our warfare are not carnal but mighty in God for pulling down strongholds, casting down arguments and every high thing that exalts itself against the knowledge of God, bringing every thought into captivity to the obedience of Christ (2 Corinthians 10:3-5 NKJV).*

Like Jesus Christ, the Apostle always works with a team. They are always strengthening and encouraging people. They are always training and bringing people into fruitfulness. They are not selfish to keep their anointing to themselves. This is because the apostolic office is not for you the Apostle, but for Jesus Christ. Thus, everyone comes to you to get encouraged to believe that you are standing for the Lord and expounding the truth of the risen Christ, and the mission of Jesus Christ for the church.

The Apostle does not live for himself as seen in these scriptures:

> *None of us lives to himself [but to the Lord], and none of us dies to himself [but to the Lord, for] (Romans 14:7 AMPC).*

The life of the Apostle is an exciting one because the Apostle is an adventurer. He loves to do something nobody has done and go places nobody has been. The apostolic anointing is not in the natural but in the spirit.

Welcome to that Spirit and Get On with the Vision

Your faith is in that vision. When you allow the faith in the Lord to work through you, you gain His love because His love is in that vision. He is in the vision. His love is in giving! Faith and Grace are, too. You see, everything about the kingdom of God always has to do with giving. But it takes the love of God to cultivate that character on a personal level so that you begin to appreciate, appropriate, and live in the full revelation of John14:12.

> I assure you, most solemnly I tell you, if anyone steadfastly believes in Me, he will himself be able to do the things that I do; and he will do even greater things than these, because I go to the Father (John 14:12 AMPC).

As an Apostle, you are expected to work the same way Jesus Christ did, and do even greater works because the same anointing is multiplied in the body. Remember what the scripture says:

> And if the Spirit of Him Who raised up Jesus from the dead dwells in you, [then] He **(the same Holy Spirit)** Who raised up Christ Jesus from the dead will also restore to life **(give life, strength, or strengthen)** your mortal (short-lived, perishable) bodies through His Spirit Who dwells in you. So then, brethren, we **(you)** are debtors, but not to the flesh [we are not obligated to our carnal nature], to live [a life ruled by the standards set up by the dictates] of the flesh **(not under the control of the flesh – senses)**.
>
>   For if you live according to [the dictates of] the flesh, you will surely die. But if through the power of the [Holy] Spirit you are [habitually] putting to death (making extinct, deadening) the [evil] deeds prompted by the body, you shall [really and genuinely] live forever. For, all who are led by the Spirit of God **(that is those who allow the**

> *Holy Spirit to direct them)* are the sons of God (Romans
> 8:11-14 AMPC, emphasis added).

Did you see that? So, by your words, you can raise the dead; by
your words you lay hands on the sick, and they shall recover (Mark
16:17-18); by your words you can prophesy. You can listen to the
Holy Spirit and do what He is instructing you. You may ask why
you should perform greater works. Understand the responsibility
to do greater works, for the Lord could come when you least
expected. For instance, you are about to have a cup of coffee, and
the Lord prompts you "Go to [a specific place] and get My words
across to the people; pray, prophesy, and show them My love for
them"

"Are you like for real, Lord? I'm about to have my coffee."

You say NO! "I am not having any of that because I am getting
my coffee and, once I get my coffee, it's time for lunch."

Can you see how the Love of the Father overrides protocols,
and disrupts your comfort and comfort zones? That is why the
apostolic is so important to develop, equip, and bring you to the
point of maturity where you will be encouraged and strengthened
to have the courage to work with the Holy Spirit

> **1 Corinthians 14:1 AMPC**
> *Eagerly pursue and seek to acquire [this] love [make it your*
> *aim, your great quest]; and earnestly desire and cultivate*
> *the spiritual endowments (gifts), especially that you may*
> *prophesy (interpret the divine will and purpose in inspired*
> *preaching and teaching).*

What does this scripture say? Follow love, but, also desire spiritual
gifts, especially so you can prophesy. That is what the apostolic

office does. Encouraging people to do what the Lord has ordained for them to do. So, what can you do? You can exalt, you can edify, you can counsel and comfort somebody. You have no need to do all the sounding brass or clanging cymbals numbers. As a matter of fact, you were already doing that while in the world before you got saved!

So, when you get to performing greater works, you are prepared because you have already built yourself up in the Love of the Father, praying in the Holy Ghost (Jude 20-21).

The Apostle teaches us to start the day with the Lord

already incorporated in our activities. Consequently, we shall continue our teaching by examining some of the responsibilities of the Apostle.

A Spiritual Front Line Ministry

Hebrew 3:1-4; I Corinthians 3:10-4:16

The Apostle represents the "Sent One" sent by a government or a high ranking official (Christ Jesus). He is the admiral of the fleet, one who has a specialized crew to go to places that are uncivilized. He is to be the architect, the builder, who would lay the foundations of a new church that would train and build a new culture – the culture of Jesus Christ. He is the one who creates an atmosphere for the truth of God's Word to be infused in the lives of others. The Apostle is also the trainer of specialists, following the model of Jesus Christ, who trained His disciples.

The Apostle as a Spiritual Passport

Ephesians 1:16:23; 3:12-21

The Apostle is the spiritual passport that permits access to the vision. The Apostle is the designated leader in the body of Jesus Christ – the church that guarantees the right passage. The Apostle has the authority, anointing, and grace to bring a Christian believer or a church into a place in the Spirit they could not access by themselves, taking them through revelation and wisdom that was impossible on their own. The apostolic anointing produces the passport, a legal document, to allow a person into new territory. The anointing on the Apostle opens new doors into the revelation of Christ Jesus, giving the opportunity to be all that the disciple was born again to be.

The Apostle is also the passport to move from the natural into the supernatural. It is the responsibility of the Apostle to transform and renew the mindset of the congregation in the knowledge of the revelation and the vision to restore the church to a mindset of the new creation that it already is (Romans 12:2-8). Verse 3 of the above scriptures, refers to the grace that was given to the Apostle. What is that grace? The grace to function in the office of the Apostle. Thus, the Apostle trains your mind to move into the spiritual realm (Philippians 4:8-9). So, quit thinking negative and quit thinking natural.

A Person Representing the Ambassador

2 Corinthian 12:12; 2 Corinthians 5:20; James 1:18-22; John 5:19-30; Romans 1:11-12

The Apostle is a special gifted messenger for Christ Jesus, who walked in Love and made faith work through Him for others. The Apostle therefore has the Spiritual Influence and Authority to speak and act on behalf of Jesus Christ. He demonstrates the patience, miracles, signs and mighty deeds of Jesus Christ with the help and leading of the Holy Spirit.

The connection between the Apostle and Jesus Christ is inseparable. Their union in the Spirit is unique, giving the Apostle the ability to move from one function to another by the leading of the Holy Spirit. His dependence on the Holy Spirit is of the utmost importance for the advancement of the Kingdom through the Body of Christ. The Apostle must be unselfish in giving all that he has to advance the Kingdom and the disciples.

A Spiritual Leader

Ephesians 3:23; Galatians 1:11-12; 1 Timothy 1:12; 1 Corinthians 15:10; 1 John 4:17-18

The Apostle is also possessed by the Holy Spirit to walk in the supernatural insight given to him by the Holy Spirit just as Jesus Christ did. This is vital for the growth and building up of the church, the Body of Jesus Christ on earth. As a spiritual leader, the Apostle recognizes in his office the wisdom and revelation to believe that, as Christ Jesus is, so also is he anointed to bring others into the same revelation (1 John 4:17). That's why patience is one of the virtues in the office of the Apostle.

Moreover, the Apostle's prayer life in the office gives him the honor always created by intimacy of bringing to maturity the character of the Gift, the disciples and the vision.

The Significance of Love in the Apostolic Office

Love is essential to the functioning of your apostolic calling to the extent that everything you do in your character is measured or judged by your love for the vision. See how Apostle Paul decries the absence of love in the ministry.

> *If I [can] speak in the tongues of men and [even] of angels, but have not love (that reasoning, intentional, spiritual devotion such as is inspired by God's love for and in us), I am only a noisy gong or a clanging cymbal. And if I have prophetic powers the gift of interpreting the divine will and purpose), and understand all the secret truths and mysteries and possess all knowledge, and if I have [sufficient] faith so that I can remove mountains, but have not love (God's love in me) I am nothing (a useless nobody). Even if I dole out all that I have [to the poor in providing] food, and if I surrender my body to be burned or in order that I may glory, but have not love (God's love in me), I gain nothing. Love endures long and is patient and kind; love never is envious nor boils over with jealousy, is not boastful or vainglorious, does not display itself haughtily.*
>
> *It is not conceited (arrogant and inflated with pride); it is not rude (unmannerly) and does not act unbecomingly.*
>
> *Love (God's love in us) does not insist on its own rights or its own way, for it is not self-seeking; it is not touchy*

or fretful or resentful; it takes no account of the evil done to it [it pays no attention to a suffered wrong]. It does not rejoice at injustice and unrighteousness, but rejoices when right and truth prevail. Love bears up under anything and everything that comes, is ever ready to believe the best of every person, its hopes are fadeless under all circumstances, and it endures everything [without weakening] (1 Corinthians 13 AMPC).

Here Apostle Paul is summing up everything regarding your activity in the church and your love for the vision. Every other assignment you engage in regarding the vision is not profitable if you have no love – the God kind of Love.

As noted above, the Apostle encourages you to do what you are equipped to do. This is why the apostolic is significant and unique as you are always encouraged to love. When the Apostle teaches you to walk in love, it is easier to flow in the gifts.

When you walk in love, the spiritual gifts flow naturally. You become a conduit for the gifts because you are connected to the source of Love. The Apostle travails in prayers for the vision. As an Apostle, you need to learn how the Apostles prayed. You can look at how Jesus Christ prayed or how the Apostle Paul prayed. As for me, I always learn from how the Apostle Paul prayed and I model my prayer life and that for the vision in line with Apostle Paul's example.

As an Apostle, I am always praying the prayers that the Apostle Paul prayed. I have learned to figure out how I can get connected to the source of the spiritual gifts, so the gift can flow through me. In the epistle of Apostle Paul to the Ephesians, the first and third chapter are the prayers he prayed for the vision. Also, in the first chapter of Colossians, is his prayer for the vision. When the congregation understands the prayer life of the Apostle and begins to embrace that prayer life, the flow is amazing.

Now, let's examine the scriptures for more inspiration and revelation on the apostolic. Listen to how important the apostolic is.

From the message of Apostle Paul to the Philippians let's look at the first chapter:

> *Grace (favor and blessing) to you and [heart] peace from God our Father and the Lord Jesus Christ (the Messiah). I thank my God (my Father) in all my remembrance of you (the new beginning. In every prayer of mine I always make my entreaty and petition for you with all joy (delight) (Philippians 1:2-4 AMPC).*

"In every prayer of mine" – can you see the heart and love of the Apostle? He says in every prayer he prays for the new beginning and the vision, he always makes his entreaty and petition for you **(the new beginning)** with all with joy (delight). Isn't that testimony a miracle?

Then in verse 5 he says,

> *[I thank my God] (my father) for your fellowship (your sympathetic cooperation and contributions and partnership) in advancing the good news (the Gospel) from the first day [you heard it] until now.*

Now watch what he said in verse 6:

And I am convinced and sure of this very thing, that He Who began a good work in you will continue until the day of Jesus Christ [right up to the time of His return], developing [that good work] and perfecting and bringing it to full completion in you (the new beginning) (emphasis added).

Beloved, that is the complete and perfect gospel. He said he was going to work until the new beginning is matured and perfected in the vision. He agreed with the word and the Holy Ghost when he said he would work until Jesus Christ came. That is the revelation of the content of the Apostle's mind in the era of the Apostle Paul. How about our time? Religion has got our mind programmed to think about the end of the world, then you go to heaven.

No, Beloved, that message is flawed, as you can see in Apostle Paul's prayers for the new beginnings. What he is saying is: "I am going to give you a testimony. I want to see the new beginning grow into maturity in the revelation, doing what it was designed to do. I am going to work in you so that you can see who you really are in the vision because, the more you see yourself, the more you see Him. The more you see Him, and the more you appreciate your value in handling the revelation and the vision as the new beginning.

In order to do greater things in the apostolic, I am going to be available to the Holy Ghost everywhere I go. Let me conclude by taking this a little further, so you see more on how the apostolic functions.

Philippians 1:7 AMPC

It is right and appropriate for me to have this confidence and feel this way about you all, (the new beginning) because you have me in your heart and I hold you in my heart as partakers and sharers, one and all with me (and in my ability) (emphasis added).

In essence, what Apostle Paul is saying is, "because you are connected to me you can share my ability." Jesus Christ said the same.

He said, "Come and I will teach you how to fish for men" (Matthew 4:19.) How do you evangelize? You evangelize (fish for men) using miracles, signs, and wonders, of grace (God's unmerited favor and spiritual blessing). *"[This is true] both when I am shut up in prison and when I am out in the defense and confirmation of the good news (the Gospel)"* (Philippians 1:7 AMPC), that is, walking in the revelation of the truth puts you in a place you can enjoy everything Apostle Paul had. The reason for this is everything Paul possesses has already been paid for. So, he spends time with the Lord to bring to you the revelation that the only way to be successful in kingdom business is to follow the instructions as given by the vision.

Remember the only way to have good success is to mediate on the word (Joshua 1:8) and that means to spend time with God.

CHAPTER SIX

CONCLUSION - MANY PARTS, ONE BODY

IT IS AWESOME TO arrive at this final conclusion on the teaching of the Five-Fold Ministry. We saw in this teaching that though the anointing and the gifts are essential aspects of the Five-Fold Ministry, our focus is on the character that is required to sustain the Five-Fold Ministry. In view of the importance of character, we shall briefly recap some basic requirements of the Five-Fold Ministry

We recognized, from the introduction, the key to understanding the Five-Fold Ministry is embodied in the words "FUNCTION" and "PURPOSE". The "Five-Fold" defines the FUNCTION rather than the focus, for those called into the Five-Fold Ministry. Therefore, it is fitting for individuals counted worthy to function in these offices (Acts 5:41-42; Hebrews 3:3) to recognize that their focus is on the responsibilities tied to the office. These officeholders require support with realigning and refocusing their attention to the functions of the offices and supervising the flock. Everybody in the vision as revealed by the Apostle Paul, is a unique member of the vision and is consequently accountable.

1 Corinthians 12:12-27 AMPC

For just as the body is a unity and yet has many parts, and all the parts, though many, form [only] one body, so it is with Christ (the Messiah, the Anointed One). For by [means of the personal agency of] one [Holy] Spirit we were all, whether Jews or Greeks, slaves or free, baptized [and by baptism united together] into one body, and all made to drink of one [Holy] Spirit. For the body does not consist of one limb or organ but of many.

If the foot should say, Because I am not the hand, I do not belong to the body, would it be therefore not [a part] of the body? If the ear should say, Because I am not the eye, I do not belong to the body, would it be therefore not [a part] of the body? If the whole body were an eye, where [would be the sense of] hearing? If the whole body were an ear, where [would be the sense of] smell? But as it is, God has placed and arranged the limbs and organs in the body, each [particular one] of them, just as He wished and saw fit and with the best adaptation. But if [the whole] were all a single organ, where would the body be? And now there are [certainly] many limbs and organs, but a single body.

And the eye is not able to say to the hand, I have no need of you, nor again the head to the feet, I have no need of you. But instead, there is [absolute] necessity for the parts of the body that are considered the more weak. And those [parts] of the body which we consider rather ignoble are [the very parts] which we invest with additional honor, and our unseemly parts and those unsuitable for exposure are treated with seemliness (modesty and decorum), Which our more presentable parts do not require.

But God has so adjusted (mingled, harmonized, and subtly proportioned the parts of) the whole body, giving the greater honor and richer endowment to the inferior parts which lack [apparent importance], So that there should be no division or discord or lack of adaptation [of the parts of the body to each other], but the members all alike should have a mutual interest in and care for one another. And if one member suffers, all the parts [share] the suffering; if one member is honored, all the members [share in] the enjoyment of it. Now you [collectively] are Christ's body and [individually] you are members of it, each part severally and distinct [each with his own place and function].

The importance of this unity in the vision is so crucial that Apostle Paul, on several instances, referred to its "oneness." His intention was to bring the flock to the knowledge of the profound revelation which is in the functioning and running of the vision as an organized living entity. Thus, in his letters to the Romans and Corinthians Apostle Paul penned the following:

Romans 12:4-6 AMPC

For as in one physical body we have many parts (organs, members) and all of these parts do not have the same function or use, So we, numerous as we are, are one body in Christ (the Messiah) and individually we are parts one of another [mutually dependent on one another]. Having gifts (faculties, talents, qualities) that differ according to the grace given us, let us use them: [He whose gift is] prophecy, [let him prophesy] according to the proportion of his faith . . .

1 Corinthians 10:17 AMPC

For we [no matter how] numerous we are, are one body, because we all partake of the one Bread [the One Whom the communion bread represents].

Can you see who you are in the vision? The mind of Jesus Christ as revealed by Apostle Paul is, though we are individuals, a part of the vision and we should see nobody else but Jesus Christ. Consequently, he wrote:

2 Corinthians 5:16-18 AMPC

Consequently, from now on we estimate and regard no one from a [purely] human point of view [in terms of natural standards of value]. [No] even though we once did estimate Christ from a human viewpoint and as a man, yet now [we have such knowledge of Him that] we know Him no longer [in terms of the flesh].

Therefore if any person is [ingrafted] in Christ (the Messiah) he is a new creation (a new creature altogether); the old [previous moral and spiritual condition] has passed away. Behold, the fresh and new has come! But all things are from God, Who through Jesus Christ reconciled us to Himself [received us into favor, brought us into harmony with Himself] and gave to us the ministry of reconciliation [that by word and deed we might aim to bring others into harmony with Him].

He continued this revelation of how the vision should be in 2 Corinthians 6:1-2 AMPC:

> *Laboring together [as God's fellow workers] with Him then, we beg of you not to receive the grace of God in vain [that merciful kindness by which God exerts His holy influence on souls and turns them to Christ, keeping and strengthening them—do not receive it to no purpose]. For He says, In the time of favor (of an assured welcome) I have listened to and heeded your call, and I have helped you on the day of deliverance (the day of salvation). Behold, now is truly the time for a gracious welcome and acceptance [of you from God]; behold, now is the day of salvation!*

Often, the problem with the Five-Fold is when we give undue attention to the designation and the bearer. That causes us to lose our focus on the Father who is the Great Father behind everyone's well-being in the ministry. Thus, in reinforcing this teaching, it becomes pertinent to examine once again our hand as the symbolic representation of the Five-Fold Ministry and the 5 Gs of Ministry. Beginning with the office of the Apostle, through the office of the Prophet, the office of the Evangelist, to the office of the Pastor and Teacher, let's review and consolidate what we already know about the vision.

The **Thumb** represents the Apostle. He generally oversees the affairs of the vision and develop the operational strategies. He is able to touch all aspects of the vision with a grip that fosters cohesiveness in the vision.

The **Forefinger** represents the Prophet – whose purpose is to guide the flock. He communicates guidance, always asking of God the next step and revealing this in the vision.

The **Middle finger** represents the Evangelist – the Dinner Bell. He gathers, reaches, and seeks souls, delivering them to the pastors for training.

The **Ring finger** represents the Pastor. He trains and leads the flock in the direction of the revelation and vision, providing sustenance and security as he directs the flock. He is forever wedded to the sheep.

The **Pinky** represents the Teacher – the Cream of the Crop. He provides balance in the vision, teaching correcting, and providing answers to queries.

The 5 Gs of Ministry

In the 5 Gs of ministry we established the following:

The Apostle "Governs" the House. He is responsible for providing the vision, he brings order to the house, develops leaders and raises "sons in the Gospel. They are "God-ward" and minister to Him. His disciples receive the vision, and then they go and plow the ground for the "harvest."

The Prophet "Guides" the House providing administration, counseling, and direction, declaring and confirming the vision of the House as the "watchman on the wall" or "crow's nest" minister.

The Teacher "Grounds," in other words, he teaches, trains, and equips the saints, bringing balance to the vision of the House. He also breaks up the fallow ground.

The Evangelist "Gathers," scavenging for souls and also sowing seeds.

The Pastor; "Guards." He is the operations officer of the House, caring for the people; overseeing visitations and the everyday aspects of the community of faith. He leads the prayer and care ministries and harvests the crop.

As the High Priest, Jesus Christ left a brilliant model for the vision (Hebrews 3:1; 4:14; 10:39). He is the Pastor, Prophet, and the General Overseer (Apostle) of the vision. He oversees the church which is His body. He is the Chief Shepherd of the flock, responsible for the nourishment and good health of the flock and the Pastors in the house must emulate His style. Jesus Christ is always in the house, even though He has risen. He serves as the midwife of the new converts, caring and nursing the babes in Christ through the Five-Fold Ministry until they become mature. Furthermore, the Chief Apostle oversees the ministers (the Five-Fold Ministry) and the church (the congregation).

The Apostle always looks out for the revelation and vision of what the Father is doing and what he wants done (John 5:19). He brings the mind of God through the fivefold to the new beginning. It could be fair to say that, while the Pastor oversees the flock, the Apostles oversees the vision. They teach the new converts how to run with the vision as revealed to them by Jesus Christ.

Recognize the pre-eminence of the office of Apostle to the vision to the extent that, even after Jesus Christ has risen, He is still working among the new converts, equipping, helping, and bringing them to the place of revelation, where they will be able to appreciate their place in the vision. Only then will they fulfill the vision and accomplish their individual responsibilities in the vision. One striking example is the road to Emmaus experience.

The Emmaus Experience (Luke 24:13-40)

When Jesus Christ rose from the grave, it was the women who first found out (Luke 24:10). The first person that saw Jesus Christ in His glorious body was Mary Magdalene from whom Jesus Christ had cast out seven demons. You see, you cannot be so broken too far that the vision will not incorporate and accommodate you.

> *Now when He rose early on the first day of the week, He appeared first to Mary Magdalene, out of whom He had cast seven demons. She went and told those who had been with Him, as they mourned and wept. And when they heard that He was alive and had been seen by her, they did not believe (Mark 16:9-11 NKJV).*

Jesus Christ then appeared to two of His disciples who, like Mary Magdalene, went to break the news to Peter and his team. But they refused to believe.

> *After that, He appeared in another form to two of them as they walked and went into the country. And they went and told it to the rest, but they did not believe them either (Mark 16:12 NKJV).*

Jesus Christ appeared to two of the disciples. Later He appeared to the eleven as they sat at the table, and He rebuked them for their unbelief and hardness of heart, for not believing those who had seen Him after he had risen (verse 14). You see how they were prone to ignore a revelation of those we consider just ordinary?

Then Jesus commissioned them to go out and preach the Gospel:

> "Go into all the world and preach the gospel to every creature. He who believes and is baptized will be saved; but he who does not believe will be condemned. And these signs will follow those who believe: In My name they will cast out demons; they will speak with new tongues; they will take up serpents; and if they drink anything deadly, it will by no means hurt them; they will lay hands on the sick, and they will recover" (Mark 16:14-18 NKJV).

Following this, He ascended into heaven where He was received (verses 19 to 20). It is instructive to observe the behaviors of those who were to carry the vision of the new beginnings to the international community. No doubt it was disheartening to realize that, after all Jesus Christ had done during His earthly life, there was still the need to pursue, love, care for, and correct the flock until they could run with the vision.

This typifies the reality of the Five-Fold Ministry: that there is no room for negligence and irresponsibility. The job must be done, and love and care are the keys. It doesn't matter the hardness of the heart of the person you bring to the Lord; you have to keep praying for them and, if they give you the audience, continue to speak to them. Travail at the altar for them, day and night, and cry out to God to give you wisdom, discernment, and strength to pursue them with the vision in divine revelation.

Now back to the to the Emmaus experience in Luke 24. Two of Jesus Christ's disciples were returning on the day of His resurrection to a village called Emmaus, which was seven miles from Jerusalem. And they talked together of all the things which had happened.

> So it was, while they conversed and reasoned that Jesus Himself drew near and went with them. But their eyes were restrained so that they did not know Him. **(This means they were not able to discern by revelation and understanding who their guest was. They were absorbed into the events of the last few hours, though their bodies gave them signs, which you will see shortly)**. And Jesus Christ said to them, "What kind of conversation is this that you have with one another as you walk and are sad?" Then, the one whose name was Cleopas answered and said to Him, "Are You the only stranger in Jerusalem, and have You not known the things which happened there in these days?" And Jesus Christ said to them, "What things?"
>
> So they said to Him, "The things concerning Jesus of Nazareth, who was a Prophet **(the disciples recognize Jesus Christ as a Prophet)** mighty in deed and word before God and all the people, and how the chief priests and our rulers delivered Him to be condemned to death and crucified Him. But we were hoping that it was He who was going to redeem Israel (Luke 24:15-21 NKJV, emphasis added).

Now, can you see the error in perception? And why the ministry of the fivefold is critical? The majority of the disciples had the mind that there was going to be a physical confrontation to liberate Israel from the Romans. What Jesus Christ had told them concerning His ministry and death did not actually register in their minds.

Do you see that they needed revelation to come to the understanding of the mystery of the blood, the death, the cross, burial, and the resurrection of Jesus Christ? So the two disciples went on telling Jesus Christ about Himself, that it was the third day since these things happened.

> "Yes, and certain women of our company, who arrived at the tomb early, astonished us. When they did not find His body, saying that they had also seen a vision of angels who said He was alive. And certain of those who were with us went to the tomb and found it just as the women had said, but Him they did not see" (Luke 24:22-24 NKJV).

Can you see the level of unbelief even among the disciples who were to head the Five-Fold Ministry? Are you beginning to see the relevance of your place that these men were just as broken and blind as most of us are today? How could they have been astonished at the resurrection of Jesus Christ when Jesus Christ had given them specific and complete details of the progression of the events before they occurred?

> Then He said to them, "O foolish ones, and slow of heart to believe in all that the Prophets have spoken! Ought not the Christ to have suffered these things and to enter into His glory?" And beginning at Moses and all the Prophets, He expounded to them in all the Scriptures the things concerning Himself (Luke 24:25-27 NKJV).

Can you see that, even though they were disciples, with knowledge of the scriptures, Jesus Christ had to go back to the basics of expounding the revelation and the vision to theNow here is the shock and inspiration.

> Then they drew near to the village where they were going, and He indicated that He would have gone farther. But they constrained Him, saying, "Abide with us, for it is toward evening, and the day is far spent." And He went in to stay with them. Now it came to pass, as He sat at the table with them, that He took bread, blessed and broke it, and gave it to them. Then, their eyes were opened, and they knew Him, and He vanished from their sight (Luke 24:28-31).NKJV

What an awesome experience! What a brilliant way to fire up His disciples and force them onto the field again! Jesus Christ kept pushing and pushing the disciples; likewise, we are to model our responsibility according to the vision and the disciples.

Jesus Christ Validates His Identity with His Scars

> And they said to one another, "Did not our heart burn within us while He talked with us on the road, and while He opened the Scriptures to us?" (Luke 24:32)NKJV

Can you see, though, they had the prompting of the unusual presence of the Risen Lord but, were too engrossed in the minutiae of the moment to grasp kingdom realities?

So, they rose up that very hour and returned to Jerusalem, and found the eleven and those who were with them gathered together, saying, "The Lord is risen indeed, and has appeared to Simon!" And they told about the things that had happened on the road and how He was known to them in the breaking of bread. Now as they said these things, Jesus Himself stood in the midst of them, and said to them, "Peace to you." But they were terrified and frightened and supposed they had seen a spirit (Luke 24:33-37)NKJV.

Beloved, can you see the relevance of this teaching of the Five-Fold Ministry? Can you observe from these proceedings that you, too, the disciples of Jesus Christ need to be reassured?

And He said to them, "Why are you troubled? And why do doubts arise in your hearts? Behold My hands and My feet, that it is I Myself. Handle Me and see, for a spirit does not have flesh and bones as you see I have." When He had said this, He showed them His hands and His feet (Luke 24:38-40)NKJV.

Now be honest. How many of you want to see the scars of Jesus Christ to be convinced? How many of you are still waiting to see the pierced hands and feet of Jesus Christ? Beloved, if that is what you need, let me propose an easier way. Ask Jesus Christ to reveal Himself to you. He will. Nonetheless, recognize now that you bear the scars of Jesus Christ. If anyone requires proof of His scars, you are what they need (Galatians 6:17). You may not bear the visible scars of beatings as Paul did, but you might bear emotional scars of a different type of persecution.

You are the Testimony of Jesus Christ

Can you see our modern apostles behaving like the disciples of Jesus Christ in unbelief? Can you see that, though we have so many claiming to be apostles, the real Apostles are in short supply and the vision needs you?

Jesus Christ, as you recognize and see from the above passage, was and still is the Chief Apostle. Even in heaven, He is still doing the work of the Apostle and oversees the apostolic calling of His new beginning in His ministry. Consequently, in the wisdom of Apostle Paul, I leave you with this interesting revelation of the calling –which is YOU!

> So then, brethren, consecrated and set apart for God, who share in the heavenly calling, [thoughtfully and attentively] consider Jesus **(emulate Jesus Christ)** the Apostle and High Priest Whom we confessed **(who we represent)** [as ours when we embraced the Christian faith] (Hebrews 3:1 AMPC, emphasis added).

Cruciality

The responsibility of the apostolic office is so crucial to the vision that Jesus Christ after His resurrection had to meet with His Apostles and disciples to encourage them. As a result, in the gospel according Mark 16:9-12, Jesus Christ revealed Himself and His glorious body to Mary Magdalene, making her the first person to see the Risen Lord. But ironically, when she went to the disciples to inform them, they didn't believe her.

This aspect of the character of the disciples exemplifies the relevance and cruciality of the apostolic ministry and the revelation of Jesus Christ.

Demonstration of the New Beginning

As I draw to a close, let me point out the relevance of the breaking of bread in the new convert for revelation and insight. Although, not an observable part of this teaching, it is definitely an element in the office of the Five-Fold Ministry, for the breaking of bread was demonstrated several times by Jesus Christ after His resurrection.

Thus, it is fair to claim that Jesus Christ broke bread more times with His disciples after His resurrection. This practice could be modeled by the Five-Fold.

Remember, the Apostles broke bread as they went from house to house, revealing for the first time the true picture of the vision of Jesus Christ (Acts 2:42-47). This characteristic demonstrates how the church which is the body of Jesus Christ should function.

Acts 2:42-47 NKJV

And they continued steadfastly in the apostles' doctrine and fellowship, in the breaking of bread, and in prayers. Then fear came upon every soul, and many wonders and signs were done through the apostles. Now all who believed were together, and had all things in common, and sold their possessions and goods, and divided them among all, as anyone had need. So continuing daily with one accord in the temple, and breaking bread from house to house, they ate their food with gladness and simplicity of heart, praising God and having favor with all the people. And the Lord added to the church daily those who were being saved.

It is my pleasure to close with this word from the Lord:

> *"My time has come to be with you, so come and be still and you will know who I Am and who you are. I chose you and I have given you all of Me so that you can be My image and likeness now in this present age of My grace. It's my love that will create everything you will ever need to be, My ambassador, My personal representative, My example and My sample. My Holy Spirit has come to cause you to move in My ministry as I did while I was on the earth. Now I have ordained and appointed you to represent me in My office.*
>
> *"If you will understand that all of the offices are Mine and you are walking in My office, the Holy Spirit will help you as He helped Me. As you yield to the Holy Spirit, He will develop My character in you to complement the free gifts that I gave you when I called you to My service. I am honored that you have accepted the calling. Now everything has been prepared and the Holy Spirit will lead you all the way to the end. Know now that Love cannot fail. I am Love and I am dwelling in you and you will not fail,"* says the Lord your Helper.

ACKNOWLEDGMENTS

I AM SO EXCITED TO finally begin to be a scribe for the Lord. I have known for years that the time would come and now it has begun. I want to thank my wife Margie for her love, support and assistance in this project. I want to especially thank my spiritual daughter Teresa McCurry for being the one to push me into my new position and adventure. I also want to thank her for her time and resources that she made available to me for the completion of this book.

My prayer is that every disciple that the Lord causes to study this first lesson will become all that they are called to be: an ambassador, personal representative, an example, and sample of Christ Jesus. It is my prayer that this book will help all disciples to discover and fulfill the vision that they have been assigned to with the help of the Master Holy Spirit.

THE CHARACTER OF THE
FIVE-FOLD MINISTRY

LOVE

Through the Lens of

About the Author

CHIEF APOSTLE LEON D. Nelson, Jr. is a dedicated man of God that loves the Lord. He gave his life to the Lord in 1981 after living a very worldly life. After nothing seemed to work for him anymore, he told a friend, "Man, nothing is working for me anymore. I think I'll try God." And so he did. He found God to be very faithful to him and now he lives his life to please Him.

Apostle Leon D. Nelson is a native of Macon, GA, where he was ordained an itinerant elder in the African Methodist Episcopal Church in 1987 after five years of training. He pastored churches in Fort Valley and Byron, GA, for over 15 years.

Pastor Nelson and his wife Margie are the founders of Embassy Ministries International, Inc. where he was elevated to the Office of Apostle. This is an Aquila and Priscilla Ministry of Helps to the Body of Christ. The vision of this ministry is to be a distribution center, both spiritually and materially, to the body of Christ, with special emphasis on mentoring husband and wife couples, as well as ministering to ministers and church leaders (like Aquila and Priscilla).

In 1996, Apostle Nelson moved to Cleveland, Ohio, to help in the vision of one of his brothers. Upon completion of that assignment, the Lord planted him at Christian Fellowship Center, where Bishop Bill and Pastor Shirley McKinney were the Senior Pastors. He and his wife served as ministerial staff there as well as marriage counselors. They were faithfully committed to both Bishop Bill and Pastor Shirley McKinney until their transition.

As an Apostle, Leon Nelson is fulfilling the mission the Lord gave him, which is to bring unity to the church leaders in Cleveland so that church leaders from everywhere will come here to see a picture of God's plan and purpose for the church in action.

In 2007 Apostle Nelson and his wife Pastor Margie began an additional work by birthing Kingdom Disciple Church. They have been commissioned to "make disciples" by shepherding those God has called to be a part of this ministry.

Apostle Nelson was further elevated to Chief Apostle Leon D. Nelson, Jr. in 2018.

Chief Apostle Nelson has been the husband of one wife, Margie, and they celebrated their 52nd wedding anniversary on December 17, 2019. They are the parents of four daughters and sons-in law, grandparents of seven, and great grandparents of three.

Chief Apostle's life scripture is Matthew 6:33 AMPC: *"But seek (aim at and strive after) first of all His kingdom and His righteousness (His way of doing and being right), and then all these things taken together will be given you besides."*

THE CHARACTER OF THE
FIVE-FOLD MINISTRY

LOVE

Through the Lens of